Auteur Theory and *My Son John*

T0353271

Auteur Theory and *My Son John*

JAMES MORRISON

BLOOMSBURY ACADEMIC
NEW YORK • LONDON • OXFORD • NEW DELHI • SYDNEY

BLOOMSBURY ACADEMIC
Bloomsbury Publishing Inc
1385 Broadway, New York, NY 10018, USA

BLOOMSBURY, BLOOMSBURY ACADEMIC and the Diana logo
are trademarks of Bloomsbury Publishing Plc

First published in the United States of America 2018

Cover design by Alice Marwick
Cover images: *Cahiers Du Cinéma* © Ronald Grant Archive /
Mary Evans, *My Son John* © Everett Collection / Mary Evans

A catalog record for this book is available from the
Library of Congress.

ISBN: HB: 978-1-5013-1175-8
       PB: 978-1-5013-1174-1
       ePDF: 978-1-5013-1171-0
       eBook: 978-1-5013-1172-7

Series: Film Theory in Practice

Typeset by Integra Software Services Pvt. Ltd.

To find out more about our authors and books visit
www.bloomsbury.com and sign up for our newsletters

Dedicated to Thomas Schur and
in memory of Dennis Turner (1946–1984)

CONTENTS

ACKNOWLEDGMENTS

At the outset of a book on this subject, it is important to note that no act of authorship is singular. Among the many people who have contributed to this project, wittingly or otherwise, I would like to acknowledge series editor Todd McGowan and Katie Gallof at Bloomsbury. Both were supportive and patient throughout, even when the enterprise had its stubborn downturns. Also at Bloomsbury, Erin Duffy and Lauren Crisp worked with efficiency and reassuring cheer. Manikandan Kuppan capably guided the book through production. All helped to keep ever-hovering anxieties to a heartening minimum.

Thanks to the Office of the Dean of Faculty at Claremont McKenna College for supporting the research of this book and to the staff of the Margaret Herrick Library, especially Jenny Romero, for facilitating it.

While he was a graduate student at Claremont Graduate University, Jonathan Dickstein provided superb research assistance in the early stages of the project. A panel on film authorship at the Modernist Studies Association meeting of 2016 allowed me to test some ideas for the book and encounter others. Thanks to Kristen Hatch, Jeff Menne, and Keri Walsh for their participation.

Karyn Sproles assented to a viewing of *My Son John* on my behalf, and the reactions she shared with me were truly galvanizing. Thomas Schur (to whom this book is dedicated), Mary Cappello, Andrea and Joe Gomez, Dante Harper, Maria Pramaggiore, and Jean Walton continue to inspire me—but what else is new? They're all so good at seeing things as they "really are," you might think they'd learned the art from Leo McCarey himself.

All information on McCarey's work and the production history of *My Son John*, unless otherwise noted, comes from files on McCarey and the film held at the Margaret Herrick Library, Academy of Motion Picture Arts and Sciences, Beverly Hills, California (abbreviated in the text as MHL).

The source for all comments on McCarey's appearance before the House Un-American Activities Committee is the transcript of his testimony at the Internet Archive: https://archive.org/stream/hearingsregardin1947aunit/ hearingsregardin1947aunit_djvu.txt (last accessed January 15, 2018).

Introduction

In *Mike Nichols: An American Master* (2016), the title personage who dominates the film as a talking head digresses from a steady patter of amusing behind-the-scenes anecdotes from his storied film career into an extended dyspeptic rumination on the critical landscape:

> The people who describe all our work to all of us often don't know what they're talking about. They are wrong. They are people—literally, people who think that expressing an opinion is a creative act. The auteur stuff—I think they were these French guys with cigarette ashes all over them, and that they basically misunderstood the whole thing. The first thing they misunderstood is the so-called pantheon of great directors, because as we know, French people have some bizarre perceptions of our movies. They think Jerry Lewis is the greatest—and, Howard Hawks is a wonderful director, but he was not the greatest director Hollywood ever knew. The guys with the cigarette ashes on them ignored our greatest directors—George Stevens, Willie Wyler, Billy Wilder—Billy Wilder not so much, he became fashionable again. But the tragedy of Willie, and Stevens, and Fred Zinnemann—these were great men, but they just weren't a part of the froggy conspiracy.

He might as well have been sent over from Central Casting to play the humble albeit vain Hollywood craftsman righteously resentful of mystic revelations from a foreign cabal—the "froggy conspiracy"—with a sinister undue influence on artistic reputations stateside. Every cliché is in place: the image of the "French guys" as the kinds of pseudo-intellectual black-garbed left-bank goateed quasi-beatniks Stanley Donen parodied in *Funny Face* (1957); the why-do-they-love-Jerry-Lewis chestnut; the mystery of the Hitchcocko-Hawksien doctrine; the unjust demotions of many a yeoman-like mensch.

The usual broadsides against "auteur theory" are based on the simple idea that it posits the director as the author of a film, a claim assailed by critics as denying the collaborative nature of cinema and maintaining a romanticized vision of individual genius around the director's role. Nichols's tirade, however, is a slam against film criticism as such. As he inveighs against the know-nothings, choice excerpts from their work appear on screen, apparently meant to seem self-evidently obtuse, from Bosley Crowther declaring *Bonnie and Clyde* (1967) "a cheap piece of slapstick comedy" in the *New York Times* to Pauline Kael proclaiming *2001: A Space Odyssey* (1968) "a monumentally unimaginative movie" in the *New Yorker*. Critics themselves joined the chorus. Renata Adler, who replaced Crowther as chief critic at the *Times*, comes on following Nichols's rant to second his emotion in the *American Master* profile. In a 2014 article on auteurism's "tunnel vision," Kent Jones provides a familiar account along the lines sketched above.[1] Jones acknowledges the impact of this approach upon film criticism and theory and concedes that auteurism has been to the great benefit of international film culture, but he finds that it left in its wake a series of critical conventions that transmuted unsuitably into a kind of default shorthand method that slighted many aspects of film as art and medium while also fixating on the supposed essential contribution of film directors. Jones's chief exhibit of this debilitating influence dates to 1976, however, from which year to this it is difficult indeed to find any defender of auteurism whose advocacy is not so tempered as to resemble quite exactly, instead, disavowal. Practitioners may be legion, especially if anyone who speaks of movie directors is an auteurist, but they too, when their backs are pressed to the theoretical wall, tend more toward sheepish apologetics than wholehearted faith or zealous boosterism.

What is it, then, about this "auteur stuff" that produces such roiling passions as those of an American master like Nichols—certainly countable as one of the "auteurs" who by common consent ushered in the New Hollywood—as well as stirring the ire of countless antagonists in the world of criticism and academic film studies, while having few proponents to call its own for over four decades? One answer is the dearth of available ideas about the nature of authorship in the cinema, a lack that could stand as a challenge to foes who might still embrace some way of delineating creative contributions in film and as welcome news to the boldest enemies of auteurism whose animosities are directed precisely against romantic myths of authorship itself, and attendant conceptions of individual genius to which the cinema should by rights have put paid once and for all. What could topple into this perplexing theoretical gap more conveniently than the hapless bogy of auteurism? From that perspective, the main offense would seem to be auteurism's having become a default option in the absence of competing claims. Another possibility is that during its brief reign, auteurism shaped a cinematic canon as ripe for revision as any, if slightly more flexible than most, one with surprising staying power since its semiofficial but always nebulous enshrinements in the late 1950s and early 1960s, in ten-best lists of France's *Cahiers du Cinéma* and in directorial rankings in England's *Movie* in 1962 and in *Film Culture* in the United States the following year. As exclusionary formations, of course, canons are usually the prerogative of the powerful. Like authorship itself, they might usefully be hindered, as both have certainly been discouraged as objects of critical interest in recent decades. Given the well-known liabilities of either, however, their persistence is vexing and fascinating; it should come as no surprise, in any case, that influences on a given canon might be especially subject to critique the more readily they can be traced and the more embattled a canon becomes.

How brief *was* this reign? It was in December of 1955 that Jacques Rivette declared the age of the auteur in the pages of *Cahiers*. This *politique des auteurs* had been a while in germination and, as contributors to *Cahiers* remarked often, it was never really defined in whole. In important ways, such definition would have been inimical to it. Still, for much of the decade it was a dominant practice of the magazine to champion directors deemed "auteurs" at the expense of those who were not. By 1963, when Andrew Sarris published his *Cahiers*-influenced rankings of directors in the American journal *Film Culture*, the partisans of auteurism at *Cahiers* had moved on to making the films of the French New Wave. Though Eric Rohmer served as editor from 1958 to 1963, when Jacques Rivette assumed that role through 1967, their contributions as writers were greatly reduced. While key figures at the magazine like Serge Daney and Jean Domarchi passionately continued following the auteurist tradition, it was clearly in decline in the 1960s and replaced by the end of the decade, under Daney's editorship, by a new dominant critical emphasis on questions of politics and ideology. Meanwhile, Sarris was making his name and taking his lumps for venturing to translate the *politique des auteurs* into the "auteur theory" in America, as contributors to the *New York Film Bulletin*, from 1960 to 1964 (including Sarris), pursued auteurism as camp and cult spectatorship, among the most fruitful and understudied critical avenues to come out of the tradition.

In England, a strain of auteurism grew from the work of aesthetically inclined contributors to *Movie* (most university-trained in literary studies), but the magazine's policy was pragmatic: Already guarding themselves by then, the editors claimed a version of auteurism that produced compelling readings of films in practice. This strain coalesced with a more politically and theoretically oriented one practiced by British writers like Geoffrey Nowell-Smith and Peter Wollen, incorporating critical methods of structuralism and flowing back toward a competing magazine, *Screen,* which made some stabs in the direction of a more politicized auteurism (Paul Willemen's work on Douglas Sirk's Hollywood style as a kind of system, for instance) but mainly turned toward High Theory under the rubric of psychoanalysis and suture, Brechtian aesthetics, and the critique of ideology. Just as structuralism caught film theorists' attention, poststructuralism was already edging its way in; in virtually a single breath, in the early 1970s, writers like Nowell-Smith and Wollen vowed that delineating the figure of the auteur was no longer a pressing critical aim—and this in new editions of books first published only a few years before in which "auteur theory" had seemed something like the main event. Their synthesis of auteurism and structuralism lasted long enough to be dubbed by the ungainly coinage *cine-structuralism*, but by the time the film theorist Brian Henderson published his scathing critique of this strain in 1973, accusing it of smuggling the author back in through a theoretical guise, few of the objects of the critique were still practicing this model, giving his assessment the effect of a weirdly belated postmortem.[2]

In a mere fifteen years, then, an idea had run its course, a rocky trajectory mired as always in its cultural and historical moments. The aftershocks are with us still, but those fault lines have visibly eroded, eclipsed by alternative mythologies. Reviewing auteurism against a history of ideas, it may come as a surprise that it was, in its heyday, scarcely a theory of film authorship at all. In its first articulations in *Cahiers,* it was a convulsive, mercurial, collective reflection on certain larger ideas about the cinema—its hierarchies of value and its relation to traditional aesthetics, as well as its determining position on a cusp between realism and modernism. The *Cahiers* writers did indeed indulge some of the romantic idealism they stood accused of, but the auteur they constructed was really an antihero, existentially beset. The auteurists perceived an occulted critical edge in Hollywood cinema that gave the lie to its affirmative character as a bastion of mass culture. Peter

Wollen comes closest to my own conception of the significance of the *politique des auteurs* in his backward look in the second edition of *Signs and Meaning in the Cinema* when he detached auteurism from the cult of personality represented by the director and suggested that what the auteur theory really argues "is that any film, certainly a Hollywood film, is a network of different statements, crossing and contradicting each other, elaborated into a final 'coherent' version."[3]

The scare quotes around "coherent" here are especially striking, since the *Cahiers* writers in the 1950s assailed traditional ideas of artistic unity (as they went on to do in their films as well). The impetus of the *politique des auteurs* was to force a belated encounter in cinema with the cultural politics of modernism—its challenges to realist assumptions, its revisionist approaches to ideas of subjectivity, its reactions to and against the changing roles of culture in the course of its mass-ification. In short, the auteur was a staunch critic of American society, a figure the auteurists conjured as an instrument in the struggle to conceive what it might mean for a film to be "modern."

The one item of consensus around "auteur theory" is that it was *not* a theory. In fact, its repudiation in the United States had everything to do with the rise of critical theory in the American academy of the 1970s through the 1990s, when the age of theory was declared at an end in many quarters and a "post-theory" period peremptorily inaugurated. As a discipline, film studies in the United States allied itself with this boom wholesale; though "auteur theory" had provided a niche for film in English departments alongside other author-centered courses, it quickly became a casualty of the theoretical turn and, hence, the quintessential instance of the passé methodology that emerging ones needed in order to construct themselves as novel. This cycle of each new "turn" declaring prior practices obsolete accounts in part for why the discipline could not maintain an understanding of auteurism as a chapter in a history of ideas relevant to it, imagining only the option of disdainful dismissals of the supposedly outmoded.

Perhaps this also explains the predictable dynamic by which the most forcefully repudiated notions continue to return over and over (think cinephilia!). Be that as it may, most courses in film theory and most of the anthologies in the field still dependably feature a unit on authorship, and the "auteur theory" still opens up avenues for exploring key questions in film theory.

The first chapter of this book attempts to show how that is the case. Though its narrative may be familiar in its broad contours, I hope these theoretical contexts will answer the modernist imperative (admittedly also outmoded) to "make it new" at least in some ways. It should be clear that this amounts in no sense to a defense of auteurism or a call for its revival. Indeed, the entrenchment of auteurism in attitudes of its day is central to its treatment here, and its principal interests and uses remain primarily historical. It is as indispensable in understanding Classical Hollywood cinema, for example, as the New Criticism is in understanding the permutations of modernist literature.

In the second chapter, we turn to a case study of auteurism through an analysis of Leo McCarey's notorious 1952 film, *My Son John*. There are many reasons for this choice. The film is noncanonical, its director occupying a strangely liminal place between being both peripheral and quite significant in discourses of auteurism as they emerged. An examination of the film thus sheds light on the vicissitudes of canon-making in the contexts of "auteur theory." The film is also itself an embattled text. It has been written off even by McCarey's admirers on various grounds. Robin Wood, for example, declares it unforgivable because it follows so directly from McCarey's testimony before the House Un-American Activities Committee (HUAC) investigating Communist infiltration of Hollywood. Wood charges that McCarey informed on colleagues in the film industry in his testimony. Though Wood finds much to admire in the film's first half, he claims that only a few moments of Helen Hayes's performance in the lead can be salvaged from the last.

The film received mixed reviews in its initial run, much of the praise owing to the putative virtues of the film's anti-Communist stance, with even negative reviews taking care not to offend that perspective. It was seen as an admirable expression of the presumed Cold War "consensus" against Communism by figures like Karl Mundt, a Republican senator who seized the pulpit of the congressional record to commend the film as one of the great pro-American movies of the era. Since then, it has gained a checkered reputation in some quarters as one of the most egregious examples of Cold War ideology in American cinema, in others as simply terrible, on the order of such a classic of "bad" cinema as *Plan 9 from Outer Space* (1959). As in that film, one of the main actors of *My Son John* (Robert Walker) died before the completion of shooting, forcing the producers into last-ditch strategies to complete the film in his absence. These included using unconvincing doubles, resorting to awkward editing effects, and splicing in footage from other films. Due in part to such desperate measures, many critics have treated *My Son John* as a grand folly, an extraordinary aberration, like James Baldwin in *The Devil Finds Work* (1976), who places it at the center of his account of the McCarthy era in cinema. Even those who see it as a failed B-movie in the vein of Ed Wood tend to grant that its badness and outlandishness place it squarely in the canons of camp.

Yet its pedigree remains unstable. Arguing for the necessity of film canons in 2004, the critic Jonathan Rosenbaum included *My Son John* in his personal pantheon of the greatest of American cinema. Unavailable for years due to its disrepute, the film was featured prominently in a McCarey retrospective at Harvard University in 2008, with a program note acknowledging its notorious red-baiting reputation but suggesting that it is ultimately a discomfiting Oedipal narrative. The notoriety of this rare screening prompted subsequent television screenings on the cable channel Turner Classic Movies (the first such broadcast since 1970), a release on digital video, a license to stream on Netflix, and an exhibition at still another McCarey retrospective at the Museum of Modern Art in 2016, enhancing the film's reputation still further in recent years.

Thus, the film's status has shifted in complex ways, making it an exemplary case for considering the ebbs and flows of auteurism. Its place in McCarey's own oeuvre is equally suggestive. As the Cold War mounted following the Second World War, McCarey came to believe fervently in the dangers of Communist infiltration. He did indeed appear before HUAC as it began its investigations in Hollywood. He was among the first to testify before the committee, campaigning to confirm the extent of the problem. McCarey was a "friendly" witness, but contrary to Wood's accusation, he did not "name names." In fact, he pointedly declined to do so because, he explained, being a Communist was not against the law. Such refusal was the main transgression before the committee; it was the major rationale for blacklisting uncooperative witnesses, and McCarey escaped the HUAC's wrath only because of his right-wing affiliations and obvious anti-Communist fervor. He also said that he did not believe Hollywood should dedicate itself to the production of anti-Communist films, making his decision to produce *My Son John* that much more complicated. The film marks a clear turn in his work, and though it obviously expresses intense personal convictions in its way, it also speaks to the alleged ideological "consensus" of its day, thus enabling reflections on the relation between an auteur's "personal" beliefs and a film's channeling of social and cultural attitudes, as well as on the common opposition between auteurism and analysis of films' political and historical contexts. Finally, its "failure" permits further consideration of the notion of the auteur as romanticized individual "genius" or masterful holder of visionary powers.

Almost every reference to McCarey in criticism notes how little attention his work has received in relation to its achievement. Wood remarks pointedly on a general critical tendency to undervalue and misunderstand his work. Stanley Cavell expects readers to be surprised "that Leo McCarey should be setting the example at all for his more famous, or more prominent, colleagues" but still deems *The Awful Truth* (1937) perhaps the "best, or the deepest" of the 1930s cycle of "comedies of remarriage" that Cavell anatomizes, and he finds McCarey's position in cinema analogous to Nietzsche's in philosophy.[4] (Maybe you had to be there?) Cavell's means of crediting McCarey derive indirectly from auteurist practice. He recalls Jean Renoir's comment that McCarey understood people better than any other Hollywood director. This oft-cited and possibly apocryphal remark recurred as a sort of certificate of legitimation, an auteurist calling card—Andrew Sarris quoted it too while escorting McCarey into an exalted position in Sarris's own rankings—suggesting how little was needed to peg an auteur, only a few tidbits, in the end. Just as Hitchcock had his childhood night in jail at his father's behest (a yarn mentioned in relation to *The Wrong Man* [1957] more times than anyone could tally), his Catholicism, his apparent penchant for cool blondes, his few repeated comments about the nature of his work like his notion of the MacGuffin, a convenient plot device on which to hang suspense set pieces, or his spiel about the bomb under the table (if we knew it was there it was suspense, if not mere shock), and so forth. McCarey too had his corresponding rounds of scuttlebutt: a reputation (largely courtesy of Charles Laughton) as a comic genius, a Catholic of Irish origins with some heavy drinking in the mix, his father an erstwhile boxing promoter and he an amateur fighter (and many of his films featuring boxing), his sister a nun (ditto the nuns in the movies, including a boxing nun in one of them), constantly naming his female leads Lucy, a waggish proposition about the funniest scene he could imagine being one in which someone at a fancy dinner party farts, and nobody reacts at all.

Though his credentials were squarely conferred, McCarey was in many ways an unlikely auteur—another reason to make him our prime example. In one sense, though, he clearly fit the bill: his career was readily divisible into clear phases, as a proper auteur's should be. In the 1920s he worked in various capacities on countless shorts produced by Hal Roach studios, principally on two popular series, the "Our Gang" and Laurel and Hardy comedies. By the beginning of the sound era, he graduated to features that extended this apprentice work by being themselves short (about an hour each), slight, breezy, quickly produced, mostly, to occupy the bottom halves of double bills. Among these productions was his first significant feature, *Indiscreet* (1931), distinguished by the presence of a major silent star, Gloria Swanson, bidding to maintain her stardom in the age of sound. This film was followed over the next five years by a series of movies similarly designed to showcase the talents of established personalities in this transitional period. These were split between other stars also making the passage from silent to sound pictures— Eddie Cantor in *The Kid from Spain* (1931), Mary Boland, W. C. Fields, and Charles Ruggles in *Six of a Kind* (1934), and Harold Lloyd in *The Milky Way* (1936)—and still others already known in other media whose film careers began with the talkies—the Marx Brothers in *Duck Soup* (1933), Mae West in *Belle of the Nineties* (1934), and George Burns and Gracie Allen, appearing with Boland, Fields, and Ruggles in *Six of a Kind*. The first film in McCarey's oeuvre that stands as a full-fledged "Leo McCarey film" was *Ruggles of Red Gap* (1935), followed in the next decade by the series of films that bear that stamp most indelibly and for which he remains best known: *Make Way for Tomorrow* (1937), *The Awful Truth*, *Love Affair* (1938), *Once Upon a Honeymoon* (1942), and his two biggest hits, *Going My Way* (1944) and *The Bells of St. Mary's* (1945).

The last two form a diptych set in Catholic parishes, both featuring an amiable, easygoing, straw-hatted priest played by Bing Crosby. In these movies, the sentimentality that hovered nearby in films like *Make Way for Tomorrow* or *Love Affair* comes to the fore. The adorable tykes of *Love Affair* who keep popping up to sing about how wishing will make it so pave the way for the sweetly streetwise urchins of the parish films who, in the words of the beloved tune from *Going My Way*, would like to swing on stars and carry moonbeams home in jars. In literal terms these were certainly McCarey's most "personal" films to that date in the sense that his own Irish Catholicism correlated with the movies' subjects. Yet both films have an elegiac streak, a submerged sense of mourning for the passing of certain humanistic values, that makes it difficult to say whether they bring an end to the director's middle period or initiate the "late style" of his remaining films: *Good Sam* (1948), *My Son John* (1952), *An Affair to Remember* (1957), *Rally Round the Flag Boys!* (1958), and *Satan Never Sleeps* (1962). *Good Sam* is the story of a compulsively generous man whose magnanimity threatens his marriage, a movie about the limits of altruism in an explicitly postwar context that harks back to McCarey's 1930s work but works up only half-hearted commitments to its residual comedy, which plays alternately as laborious or enfeebled. After *My Son John*, his next two films seemed to perform a penance of sorts—a remake of his own *Love Affair* and a bawdy Cold War satire. Even so, his last film, *Satan Never Sleeps*, returned insistently to anti-Communist dogma, an almost perversely obstinate declaration of where the director's true allegiances lay in the end.

Staples of auteurist approaches, overviews like this should be trusted only to the point at which any narrative is subject to doubt. Like many examples of the genre, this one traces a career of classical proportions and definable segments with meaningful turns, from an early apprenticeship of yeoman labor through a middle stretch of thriving production to a late period of consummate mastery or gradual decline, or (as is often the case in auteurist criticism) some combination of both. As a thought-experiment, this sketch aspires to the auteurist imperative to conceive of a director's body of work as cumulative and cross-referenced, guided by feedback mechanisms of a sort, with later films "answering" earlier ones and certain works positioned as reversions to prior strains, or retrenchments following seeming detours. If such a model proves insufficiently responsive to historical determinations—since the "career," in such accounts, typically emerges as self-contained, autonomous as no occupational trajectory has ever really been—that fault might always be mitigated in practice, through the critical analysis of individual works, however these might themselves always be in the process of being drawn back into the ebb and flow of the "career," the indexed character of which presumably guards against too much certainty about the place of any single instance within the flux of the whole. *Was* anti-Communism really where McCarey's "true" allegiance ultimately lay? Does a final point define a previous arc? Despite its own reputation for bolstering some "essential reality," auteurism finally complicates the idea of fixed interpretation and ultimate estimations, refusing—both as values and as concepts—the claims of organic unity and integral meaning.

Notes

1 Kent Jones, "Critical Condition," *Film Comment* (March/April 2014). https://www.filmcomment.com/article/auteur-theory-auteurism/ (accessed October 10, 2017).

2 Peter Wollen, *Signs and Meaning in the Cinema* (London: British Film Institute, 2013), 144. For another treatment of auteurism that has influenced the present study, see James Naremore, "Authorship, Auteurism, and Cultural Politics," in *An Invention Without a Future: Essays on Cinema* (Berkeley: University of California Press, 2014), 15–32.

3 Brian Henderson, "Critique of Cine-Structuralism,"in *A Critique of Film Theory* (New York: Dutton, 1980), 201–233.

4 Stanley Cavell, *Pursuits of Happiness: The Hollywood Comedy of Remarriage* (Cambridge: Harvard University Press, 1984), 231.

CHAPTER ONE

Auteurism and Film Theory

Film authorship in theory and practice

Questions of authorship have been put to the test in theory at least since the New Criticism. This was a movement in English criticism that aspired to reform culture by reforming reading, to give the practice of reading a rigor and autonomy to match that ascribed to the literary monuments under scrutiny. To this end, though the movement was peopled by scholars and practitioners alike, the figure of the author was forcibly demoted, with a series of prohibitions forbiddingly initiated to render that figure remote and to prevent any untoward interest in authorial activity that might eclipse attention to the work itself. By the time the reader encountered the book the author's part was done, after all, the author nowhere to be seen on the critical landscape; what mattered was what was indisputably present—that is, the page and its inscriptions. The Victorians in the person of John Ruskin had already postulated the "pathetic fallacy" to name the regrettable penchant of writers to project their sentimental fancies upon the natural world. Under the sponsorship of the New Critics, a host of such fallacies cropped up: the "intentional fallacy" counseled the futility of recovering intentions (as opposed, oddly, to effects of "conscious will") from the text itself, the "biographical fallacy" declared the naivety of conflating the writer's life with the work, and the "affective fallacy" commanded that one shall not assume an intense emotional reaction to be any indication of high value, as the very opposite is likelier to be the case.

The New Critics have gone the way of the Sophists, even their most promising contribution of insisting on close reading having been called sternly into question by proponents of so-called distant reading. Few need now to be instructed that fields of cultural production are far from autonomous, their products interlaced in such complicated meshes that they can hardly be seen at all apart from that vertiginous matrix. A broader and more resonant challenge to categories of authorship derived from the modern critique of the self, which also, on all of its fronts, swept the boards of critical deliberation as theory gained its berth in the academy. The psychoanalytic doctrine of the split self, divided at least by the rent between its conscious and unconscious operations, and the Marxian axiom of alienation with its post-Marxist cognate, via Louis Althusser, of the interpellated "subject" formed a foundation of much theoretical thought in the last half of the twentieth century, with powerful effects on concepts of authorship. Althusser merged the tracks, in a sense, as his ideas about Ideological State Apparatuses drew inspiration from the post-Freudian psychoanalytic thinker Jacques Lacan. For Lacan, according to most commentators, the subject neither originates language nor operates as its master; rather, the subject is constituted *by* language. In turn, language speaks ideology and vice versa, making the self's interpellation into the social order and transformation into the "subject" inevitable.

Roland Barthes's essay "The Death of the Author" (1967) took its place in a line of texts announcing the passing of cultural phenomena that still abided even as the said proclamations were relayed. The successive deaths of opera, tragedy, the novel, and other lingering formations had already been heralded with varying degrees of desolation or celebration. The *Cahiers* writers flirted with the death of cinema in their writing of the 1950s, and Jean-Luc Godard's film *Contempt* (1963) contained a bold title that read, "It is the end of cinema." Godard seemed never to tire of the formulation. Two years later, he answered a questionnaire about the state of the art from *Cahiers* with the deadpan aphorism, "I await the death of Cinema with optimism." Two years after that, he ended another film, *Weekend*, with the even blunter title "End of cinema," and in 2011, he issued a postmortem for the Fabulous Invalid that was Cinema, which had by then apparently expired once and for all, perhaps in a suicide pact with the auteur, who was simultaneously declared DOA. All that was left was for Godard to say *Goodbye to Language* (2014), as he did in his subsequent film of that name.

These proclamations had a dirge-like overtone even when they really were optimistic and actually did welcome the projected demise of the fading figment in question. In this, Barthes's text differs; it boasts the belly-fire of the recent convert. A document of Barthes's transformation from dyed-in-the-wool structuralism to an equally zealous strain of post-structuralism, the essay appeared in a pivotal year in the more general transition between these paradigms. From Vladimir Propp's morphology of folktales through Claude Lévi-Strauss's anthropological excursions, structuralism had dedicated itself to discovering stable cores of meaning in recurrent patterns of expression, a sameness in the workings of "articulate thought" among people even across radically different cultures. For Propp, if a motif appeared in a tale, pursuant ones followed predictably like the hardwired narrative codes they were taken to be; for Lévi-Strauss, myths were the sterner stuff that resolved the bothersome contradictions of life. Early work by thinkers such as Jacques Derrida and Michel Foucault had already challenged many of these presumptions, and the political upheavals in France of May 1968 led partisans to renounce Lévi Straussian "sameness" in favor of an avid embrace of difference—human differences, that is, of class, of gender, of race, of sexuality, of possibilities unknown. The very ideas of social and political progress became identified with this broad tenet, with the newly christened poststructuralists leading the charge on the intellectual flank. Derrida published *Writing and Difference* in France the same year "The Death of the Author" appeared. Derrida's book showed a heavily linguistic, even hermetic, bent in its conviction that meaning in language is differential rather than referential—that is, that words gain meaning due to their differences from other words in the linguistic system rather than from their reference to external realities—but later readers understood it as a more direct product of its political moment and of this new valorization of human variations than was initially apparent.

Barthes's books *On Racine* (1963) and *Elements of Semiology* (1964) are shot through with structuralist assumptions, but "The Death of the Author" marks a turn away from them. In fact, the essay's guiding assumption is that the Author is the purveyor of sameness, who must be condemned to extinction in order to release the inspiriting abundance of differences that await their liberation. The "birth of the reader," as the essay's famous last line would have it, "must be at the cost of the death of the Author."[1] In this formulation, the reader is the salutary citizen long held hostage and craving ultimate emancipation, with the Author as the holder of power, who might relinquish it voluntarily if threatened—as in the case of modernist writers reacting against perceived cultural decline who claimed to be eschewing personality rather than expressing it—but who must be quelled altogether if the reader is ever to be granted her own full power to read freely. The text has no singular, monolithic meaning, Barthes declares, laying waste at once to a basic structuralist credenda and to the monological "message" of the Author-God. Rather, it is a multifarious site in which different writings contend, none originating with the text in question, a tissue of reference points derived from myriad cultural sources. This definition is surely as open, as comprehensive, as malleable, as eclectic as one could hope—and as evocative of the nature of textuality in the postmodern age, assuming that modernism/postmodernism were chugging along on roughly the same timetables as structuralism/poststructuralism. If the

Author had to be a casualty in the ascendancy of this manifold understanding of textuality, how many concerned parties would hesitate to make the sacrifice?

Yet Barthes's frames of reference in "The Death of the Author" are parochial, limited to a few French classics and moderns—Balzac, Flaubert, Baudelaire, Mallarmé, and Proust—with reference to a single English writer (De Quincey) to season the discourse with a more continental flavor. None of this prevented a gathering poststructuralist chorus from hailing the essay's wholesale applicability, quite as if the choristers had not after all dispensed with the universalism they were supposed to have just repudiated. Barthes speaks only of "literature," but his use of the word "text" here takes in a wider field of transmission than one consisting only of writing qua *writing* (though Barthes otherwise uses no other word and suggests that even if "the Author" is dead writers still flourish). This slide enabled hectic generalizations from Barthes that would continue for the coming decades in the reign of deconstruction, one of post structuralism's most prominent spin-offs. Not only was the Author who had once tugged opulent forelocks and brandished quill-bedecked fountain pens in the throes of tortured genius no longer extant; even the ink-stained hacks of mass culture, purveyors of lowbrow radio plays and TV dramas, hucksters of advertising copy, posters of grimy leaflets, distributors of broadsides and pamphlets, mounters of garish billboards, producers of trashy films were reported among the departed.

The explosion of writing (or should we say text-production) in various forms following the advent of mass literacy was certainly one factor that eventually called forth the pronouncements of authorial death, even when these turned out to be more prescriptive than diagnostic. How could this dizzying scope of new activity in mass societies that boomed under the name of writing, from the pulp fictioneers of yore to the "content providers" of the digital dawn, all interface under the aegis of such an august singularity as the sign of the Author? This question seems to be what Michel Foucault, not to be outdone, had in mind in his own contribution to the burgeoning field in 1969, where he spoke of the "author-function" instead of the Author. "[C]riticism and philosophy took note of the disappearance—or death—of the author some time ago," Foucault notes, coolly divesting Barthes of his scoop.[2] "[I]n a civilization like our own," he goes on, "there are a certain number of discourses endowed with the 'author function' while others are deprived of it."[3] He cites private letters, contracts, and anonymous leaflets as texts denied the author-function while higher-order texts are "endowed" with it, implying a surprisingly traditional concept of authorship.

Just as Barthes's world is a bright horizon of bristling textuality, so Foucault's is fraught with ubiquitous, endlessly thrumming discourses, most of which figure as mere noise. In such an atmosphere of swirling communications, when we are confronted routinely by what seem to be literally author-less texts, even those that forgo anonymity and claim some expressive value seem worthy only of a downgraded designation, bureaucratic and impersonal, more befitting a postindustrial, instrumental, institutionalized order like those of modern societies.

Reading these manifestos ungenerously, one might conclude that Barthes—taking Oscar Wilde's "The Critic as Artist" (1891) a step further—aims to glorify the critic (with the reader as expedient stand-in) above the author, while Foucault, far from denigrating the Author, reestablishes the primacy of that figure as a special case amid a harrowing welter of all-purpose discourse. (Who, after all, when those select discourses are "endowed" with the "author function," does the endowing?) In fact, though these ideas trickled down to just about every cultural precinct, both Barthes and Foucault attended not to the humble denizen of mass culture but the Author of high-art lore in whom cultural authority inhered without question, and both registered (not, indeed, for the first time) modern challenges to that very authority. What kills off the mythic bogy of the Author is the same thing that brought about the well-publicized demise of high culture itself—namely, the democratization of authorship, as a by-product of the democratization of culture. This correlation is especially clear looking back from the age of the internet, when every other blogger proudly identifies as a "published author" unless he or she (unwittingly induced by Barthes at fifty removes) is too humble to claim such a laureled mantle; and when the formerly exalted cultural gatekeepers, once protectors and custodians of the Author's insular privilege, have been reduced to their proper station as minions of an everexpanding marketplace. That these declarations of the author's death were issued in the name of democratization just as what we might call author-positions expanded to become incomparably more inclusive than ever before is a paradox equal to the persistence of authorship as a paradigm even after the last gasp of the funeral march.

All of these considerations enter into thinking about authorship as a paradigm even before we arrive at the special problems of film, including its collaborative nature and its communication on multiple tracks, audial or visual. Indeed, films could be seen as the quintessential modern author-less texts, the ultimate challenge to the authorship paradigm, though they could just as easily be seen as having multiplied new and different forms of authorship in dynamic relation to one another through a democratic medium. To consider directors as singularly responsible for films would be a proposition so obviously untenable that, in fact, nobody ever held it; the fiercest proponents of auteurism have always been the quickest to dismiss any such notion as naïve or silly, even if they harbored no qualms whatever about outmoded humanisms and language speaking the subject or any of the rest of it. "Auteur theory" undeniably forestalled development of the ideas about collaboration or collective authorship that might have replaced it, though no such theory took hold in the sixty years of film history before anyone started talking about auteurs either. In recent years, the most compelling critics of auteurism still concede its galling staying power. Richard Dyer states that he never really "believed" in film authors, cinematic representation being so fraught with tangled influences and manifold kinds of meaning, but that he began to think it was necessary to come to terms with the concept in order to think about the work of gay and lesbian filmmakers. Jane Gaines similarly sees the lurking dangers of recourse to figures of authorship, especially in pedagogical terms. Where directors are taught as structures, they may still be perceived as authors. The only reason the question lingers at all, for her, is because the recovery of the work of a Dorothy Arzner or Oscar Micheaux—both missions fairly well accomplished—still seems to require some configuration of authorship to realize itself.[4]

Should the author paradigm, then, be limited to the canon-busting reclamation of women, queers, or directors of color? If it is somehow necessary for that project, must it not have other viable theoretical uses? Arzner's work provides a crucial example because it went so often against the grain. A film like *Craig's Wife* (1936) is especially instructive, providing the liberating spectacle of a director undermining the sexist premises of her material, a play by George Kelly about a woman who values her home as a showplace above the love of her husband. First produced shortly after women gained the right to vote in the United States, the play demonizes the figure of Harriet Craig as an example of the perils of women's empowerment. Through precise shifts in the material and complicated maneuvers of staging, among other techniques, Arzner exposes the title character's vulnerability and shows her longing for emancipation to be a legitimate—indeed, necessary—desire, transforming her from the compulsive dragon lady most productions portrayed into a movingly sympathetic figure. In a key scene of the play, for example, Harriet confides to a niece that she does not harbor "romantic illusions" about marriage, thinking of it instead as an avenue for women toward "emancipation" and "independence" (obviously loaded words in this context). The script demands that these lines be delivered surreptitiously so that we will understand them as symptoms of Harriet's manipulative, cunning nature: "She turns and glances up the stairs, to assure herself that no one is listening," according to the stage directions.[5] In the film, Arzner places the dialogue in public on a train and places the figure of a man in a seat behind Harriet and the niece, sitting between them as they talk with his back to them. Combined with the smothered yet irrepressible warmth of the actor playing Harriet (Rosalind Russell), the pointed interposition of the man shows how the discourse between the women continues to be mediated by male prerogatives—the man is positioned in the frame such that we expect him to turn and address them at any moment—and that Harriet's thoughts about independence are being expressed openly and directly, without concern for being overheard, even by men. Misogyny and proto-feminism clash here in the same film, in complicated ways, with the latter coming out on top to exhilarating effect, thanks to the creative interventions of a resourceful director.

The "warmth" of Rosalind Russell reminds us that the director's work always plays in tandem with multiple intersecting facets. One can easily make this case from Russell's performance in *Craig's Wife* itself, but it is aided immeasurably if one has seen Russell in, say, *My Sister Eileen* (1942), *Picnic* (1955), or *Auntie Mame* (1958), in all of which Russell's tart exterior conceals a poignant tenderness just beneath the surface. Star discourses have usually noted how our familiarity with the range of a star's performances inflects our reactions to a specific instance, so it is not surprising that rich and imaginative film interpretations often turn similarly upon awareness of a director's body of work. Indeed, auteurism implies an inter-textual understanding of film, highlighting the criss-crossing reference points that define our relation to any text, denying the integral specificity of the individual work and asserting its embeddedness in networks of meaning, including the contents of filmmakers' oeuvres.

In the case of a piece of art cinema like Carl Dreyer's *Ordet* (1955), where authorship has traditionally been less embattled, such awareness can also condition basic understanding. In the last scene of the film, a woman who has died giving birth to a stillborn child is brought back to life by an act of faith. In the beautiful last shot, she embraces her husband, who has previously been agnostic but has regained faith through the miracle of her resurrection. The shot is a medium close-up infused with molded light, suggesting an aura around them yet also a sense of encroaching darkness, and it has an intense carnality due to an intricate sound design that allows us to hear the woman's breath and both characters' skin and clothing making intimate contact. The scene is typically read as joyous, celebrating a beloved character's miraculous return from the dead. Viewers familiar with the severe and eloquent ironies of Dreyer's work, however, in his endings in particular, might sense a tragic countercurrent. The woman asks where their son is, not knowing he has died. The husband replies, "He is with God." The wife repeats, "With God?" The husband takes her question to refer to his own restored faith, and he affirms passionately that he now believes in God because of the miracle of her rebirth. He understands her response as an expression of emotion at his renewed faith. Especially considering the scene in the context of Dreyer's work, however, we may understand that she is instead reacting to the news that her baby has died, with a grief that the husband fails to perceive through the scrim of his own elation. This disconnection casts a tragic shade over the last shot that places it in line with the similar tones of the devastating final shot of Dreyer's earlier *Day of Wrath* (1943).

To conjure an author is to engage in a fantasy of sorts. It may enact a fantasy of power, with the auteur cast as the one in control, the one with the authority to decree, and the spectator taking vicarious pleasure in entering into this compact. Certainly, by the time auteurist status becomes a branding op in the New Hollywood and after, power fantasies figure prominently in constructions of the filmmaker as a dynamic maven with free reign and a "vision"—a figure of likely envy to modern subjects thoroughly apprised, courtesy of Foucault and others, of their own curtailed agency. If the author can survive so many assaults, some kind of pleasure must be at stake; an impulse to commune with this figure of the author must reflect a desire strong enough to persist even after its liabilities have been absorbed. It is an act of identification across the symbolic spaces of texts, with an imagined, spectral figure beckoning there, across, before, beyond, or within those spaces. The banishment of the author amounts to a critical prohibition against this pleasure and against the naivety of conceiving the author as a positive presence. But much more than in the cases of movie stars or characters within the fiction, encounters with authors entail identifications with an absence. In other words, this pleasure has an implicit negative basis. Even if this identification has a positive end—admiration for artistic achievements, for instance—it turns on an empty junction. Authorial communication through fictive texts is indirect by definition, and the work of film directing happens always somewhere else, other than "in" the text, even if signs of it can be traced. As we will see, to reify this tracing as an index of the ineffable is one thing auteurism was about. The auteur may have been the elusive figure in the carpet, but at least in its initial formulation the auteur's "power" was a dubious value indeed.

The *politique des auteurs* was instituted as an editorial program at *Cahiers du Cinéma* by the end of 1955, intended to identify and support directors who would be distinguished on several criteria from others by virtue of the designation of "auteur." Though the policy was never official, it was embraced by the magazine's best-known contributors including Claude Chabrol, Jean-Luc Godard, Jacques Rivette, Eric Rohmer, and Francois Truffaut, who went on to form the core of the French New Wave of filmmaking in the 1960s. The origins of the policy are usually traced from Alexandre Astruc's idea of the camera-pen—the notion that the film director should use the camera as an instrument of personal expression just as the writer does a pen—through Francois Truffaut's "A Certain Tendency of the French Cinema."[6] The latter, however, is really an assault on the so-called "Tradition of Quality" in French cinema and a brief against slavish fidelity in film adaptation, with no mention of auteurs or Hollywood cinema.

In fact, the magazine had a long-standing stake in these questions, having devoted significant space to covering the activities of the International Federation of Film Auteurs since its founding in 1952. Its members declared themselves auteurs, using the word in a heightened sense that implied not just authorship but a larger responsibility for being custodians of film art. One of the group's main goals was to promote connections between emerging art cinemas and mainstream production. As this guild of film professionals expanded across national boundaries, some controversy arose because of differences among copyright laws from country to country. It should be remembered, however, that this matter was of less controversy in France, where the film director was and is routinely registered as author for copyright purposes, though usually in a context of joint authorship. In the United States, the producer is registered as author, with writers and directors understood as producers' agents or employees and usually excluded from authorial claims. This is largely because American laws deem authorship tantamount to ownership. Across much of Europe, meanwhile, the idea of the film producer as author was rejected in case law from the 1930s on. Films came to be understood as composite works, like anthologies with multiple contributors, usually assuming that the director, writer, and composer of original musical scores were coauthors, no matter what their employment arrangements. The only contributors clearly excluded from claims to authorship were actors, their activity understood as dictated by the script and director. "Moral rights," an important component of copyright in Europe that barely exists in the United States, had been implicit for decades and were securely granted to the director as author in France from 1957 on, with producers explicitly denied moral rights to authorship. According to Pascal Kamina, the most authoritative scholar on European film copyright, the director is the only contributor who is always recognized as the author in most current European copyright law, a circumstance he deems a direct consequence of the ideas about film authorship developed in France in the 1950s.[7]

Though these legalistic definitions hardly settle questions of authorship, they remain important backgrounds for the *politique des auteurs*. They were debated in the pages of *Cahiers* before Rohmer and company signed on, in articles by the screenwriter Louis Chavance and the filmmaker Marcel L'Herbier, among others. Chronicling the Federation of Film Auteurs, Chavance proclaimed that "the reconciliation of scenarists and directors was a first step toward an international union of auteurs," while L'Herbier, affiliated with the French Society of Film Auteurs since the 1920s, lobbied on behalf of the director.[8] As the *politique* took hold, the magazine welcomed film professionals of all stripes to its pages to refute the claim that the auteur was a mere theoretical invention and to confirm the existence of auteurs in the real world, as in the actor Pierre Bertin's moving tribute to Jean Renoir. After working on Renoir's film *Elena and Her Men* (1956), Bertin proclaimed Renoir a prototype and the quintessential auteur.[9]

A number of other strains that would animate the *politique des auteurs* preceded the arrival of the "Young Turks" who took it up with the most gusto. Jean Quéval used the word "auteur" in its *politique* sense as early as 1951 in an article against creative conformity, while Jean Myrsine contributed an article on Gene Kelly as "Auteur and One-Man Band" the year after.[10] The latter piece also indicated the magazine's already intense enthusiasm about special corners of Hollywood cinema, an ardor that became a mainstay of the *politique*. Contributors since the magazine's founding had always been especially interested in Hollywood movies that countered the affirmative character of mass culture and offered a critical view of American culture and society, a preference that fed directly into the *politique*. For example, Jacques Doniol-Valcroze found in *Come Back, Little Sheba* (1952) a "very different image of American life than the official version," one that was "neither optimistic nor paradisiacal."[11] The death-of-the-author and death-of-cinema discourses that weave through auteurism are also prefigured in Michel Dorsday's bluntly titled "The Cinema is Dead" with its dunning, redundant lead or Chris Marker's prediction of the death of Hollywood from the "gigantism" of new technologies like CinemaScope and 3D.[12]

The policy was hardly, then, a bolt from the blue, but the backlash began as soon as it was established. The denunciations were in nearly every detail the ones that would shadow the *politique* doggedly through the years of its uneasy transmutation into a theory. *Cahiers* itself printed one of the first, an unrelenting pan by the critic Barthélémey Amengual, a sometime *Cahiers* contributor with closer associations to the competing publication *Positif*. His diatribe is worth quoting at length:

> The most irritating paradox of the *Cahiers du Cinéma*, at least of the Young Turks, takes a critical attitude, contradictory only in appearance, before the films they love. Firstly, they approach the works as if they were meteorites come from heaven, self-sufficient, bearing within themselves their end and their beginning, complete worlds, perfect monads, whatever confidence the critic has to define the work's own reports, its certainties, its illusions, its similarities and values ... They burn incense by the handful to filmmakers to whom they attribute, without blinking and without restraint, the absolute paternity of the least detail, the puniest allusion, the most fleeting action ... and this, although they obviously ignore the fact that it is not very far from the producer's cup to the director's lip, at least as much in Hollywood as elsewhere. All intentions fall when they serve to build a metaphysics, to compel a style, to consolidate a vision of the world.[13]

Rohmer mounted a mild defense, writing that the *politique des auteurs* was simply "a slogan seized on the rebound" that "circulates here as well as in the opposite camp" and provides a "different framework from the system of our detractors."[14] He points out that in other arts single pieces are routinely subordinated in criticism to whole oeuvres and that film directors are given a place of honor in credits and on posters in any case, submitting that *Cahiers* draws more attention to collaborators than other film magazines. As for the auteur, the "absolute authorship of any small detail" is "not given to him at the same time as his business card": The movie is "to him an architecture of which the stones are not—must not be—born from his own flesh. Nobody denies him the right to engrave his name on the base of the monument, even if he did not handle the trowel or the cord."[15] Rohmer does not address Amengual's most striking and prescient point, the "paradox" of the auteurists' "critical attitude" toward many of the works they allegedly idolized.

Bazin, realism, and modernism

The *politique des auteurs* was just one of the principles that guided the *Cahiers* critics in the 1950s. Despite the differences of inflection from writer to writer, contributors across the masthead shared allegiances, commitments, and theoretical concerns, producing a body of writing striking in its consistency. Perhaps most clearly, these "Young Turks" articulated a distinctive critical practice informed by a theory of film under the obvious influence of André Bazin but also showing palpably (to echo the well-known phrase of Harold Bloom) the anxiety of that influence. If it had a precedent, their writing recalled the sophisticated, sometimes jocular discourses on cinema of the European avant-garde in the 1920s and 1930s charged with the impassioned cinephilia that Jean Epstein brought to the fore in that tradition. Likewise, the *Cahiers* critics approached a popular art virtually defined by simplicity, transparency, and mass appeal from the perspective of an explicitly modernist self-consciousness, with the torsion between these levels giving their work some of its headiest energies. In sum, this work amounts to a restive inquiry into the nature of the modern, with the cinema posited as its quintessential manifestation.

As editor of *Cahiers du Cinéma*, Bazin curated the writing of this new generation of young critics that would come to characterize the aesthetic of the magazine in the 1950s even more than Bazin's own definitive contributions. Bazin's essays of the 1940s had done much to consolidate film criticism as a respectable pursuit in postwar French intellectual circles, as his early work appeared in high-profile outlets of the time like *Esprit* and *L'Observateur*. As early as 1943, a version of his classic essay "The Ontology of the Photographic Image" was included in a special issue on visual culture of the Leftist journal *Confluences* alongside the work of modernists like Jean Cocteau and Gertrude Stein. The essay's title suggests Bazin's tactic to elevate film writing through recourse to theoretical, philosophical, even scientific terms of art, a strategy that recurs in pieces such as "The Entomology of the Pin-Up Girl" (1946) and, with its Darwinian reverberations, "The Evolution of the Language of Cinema" (1950–55). This commitment to a theoretical exploration of the nature of cinema—even if often in the guise of journalism—was what made Bazin's work such a fertile model for the next generation, despite their ultimate deviations from Bazinian orthodoxy.

Bazin's own influences passed to his erstwhile apprentices in mutated, revisionist forms. In particular, the work of Jean-Paul Sartre was an avowed influence on Bazin that transformed into a version of pop-existentialism in auteurist writing and, later, in the French New Wave. Though the extent of this influence on Bazin is difficult to trace, it is implicit throughout his work and quite explicit in a passage like this, recalling the founding existentialist mantra: "Cinema's existence precedes its essence," Bazin states in the key essay "In Defense of Mixed Cinema."[16] Even though Sartre himself famously declared that (as the title of an important essay had it) "Existentialism is a Humanism," he influenced Bazin most through his *less* existentially inclined work, such as his early work on emotion or his *Psychology of Imagination* (1940). Indeed, despite his own occasional protests, Sartre has usually been assigned to skeptical traditions of philosophy that are harder to reconcile with Bazin's Christian humanism, though much less so with the auteurists' brash agnosticism. Sartre does not deny "essence" in his blunt slogan; he merely grants "existence" a priority that necessarily re-conditions our ideas about essence. In practice, his stands against philosophical idealism incline him to suspect the idea of essence in any nonmaterial way, especially as a stand-in for the human soul (which is how it had commonly been construed in earlier philosophical practice). Bazin's methodical, inductive approach, inferring theoretical principles from accumulated examples, also implies a materialist orientation in its way, yet—like the other avatars of classical film theory—he remains tireless in his efforts to uncover the "essence" of cinema. In "Evolution" he considers at length the proposition that film editing constitutes its essence before rejecting it in favor of the deep-focus shots of long duration that were emerging as he wrote in the films of Jean Renoir, William Wyler, Orson Welles, and others.

In light of the enhanced depth-of-field techniques of the 1940s, Bazin argues that the cinema reaches its apotheosis and achieves a heightened realism. In short, he claims that long takes with perspectival compositions develop cinematic realism simply *because* they exclude editing, thus eliminating temporal manipulation, reproducing "real" time, and enabling spectators to explore the image without overt prompting from filmmakers who intrusively direct the viewer's gaze shot by shot. This last point has clear implications for questions of cinematic authorship, expressing a preference for the effacement of the filmmaker's presence. Indeed, the directors Bazin most admires are those he casts as humanists deemed modest enough to stand aside and allow cinematic spectacles to unfold at least in part of their own accord. The improvisatory spirit of a Chaplin, the spontaneity of a Renoir, the observational stances of Vittorio De Sica—these were the qualities Bazin celebrated, while chiding even Welles, for all his commitments to long takes and deep focus, for his periodic reversions to an unseemly expressionism. For Bazin, perhaps following Sartre's critique of determinism, a film should be influenced by the filmmakers' consciousness but not wholly determined by it. In Bazin's film theory, as Dudley Andrew puts it, cinematic space "remains partly independent of the artist who delivers it to us."[17]

Andrew further notes that to characterize Bazin as an unreconstructed idealist and a naïve realist—a view especially widespread in film theory of the 1970s and 1980s—is oversimplified at best. One of Bazin's most extended treatments of realism in film, "An Aesthetic of Reality" (1948), turns on a pungent paradox that realism can only be achieved through artifice. As that essay makes clear, Bazin's take on realism is hardly in line with the nineteenth-century versions. Indeed, a crucial section argues that the most conventional of films bears affinities with the most advanced examples of modern literature because a film is, by definition, always a sequence of fragments, while a literary work must resort to specialized techniques or procedures (a la John Dos Passos or William Faulker) to achieve such effects. Moreover, the coordinates of Bazin's realism are not objectivity, omniscience, and linear narration, but ambiguity, abstraction, and contingency— elements much more in keeping with the antirealism of modernist aesthetics.

Nor can Bazin be called an unequivocal partisan even of the realism he espouses, as he typically approaches the term with caution, often equips it with scare quotes, and acknowledges competing definitions, no one of which can achieve ultimate preeminence; even when he speaks more categorically, distinguishing "true realism" from "pseudo-realism," his treatments of the terms remain complex and even ambivalent. From his earliest work, he regards the concern for realism in the arts as a kind of fetish, even as his own fascination with cinema derives in large part, at least initially, from the ways that the photographic bases of the medium revive such concerns. In the final version of "Ontology of the Photographic Image," he speaks of the obsession with realism as if it were an unwholesome fixation, and seems to welcome the crisis in realism brought on by the rise of modernism, which challenged its claims to objectivity. Yet Bazin understood that this thirst for realism is never to be quenched, and in this and other senses, Bazin's realism is a curiously modern one, rooted in the uncertainty principle of reality itself (its "ambiguity") and in the Sartrean freedom of the individual subject to interpret at will. Though Bazin devalues those cinematic traditions that collude most closely with international modernism, like German Expressionism and Soviet Montage in the 1920s, he also pursues a parallel interest in cinema and modernity that becomes increasingly significant in his late work.

One of Bazin's last essays for *Cahiers* is a poignant tribute to Humphrey Bogart upon his death. There, Bazin locates a "'modern' character of the Bogart myth" in a "Baudelairean sense," and declares Bogart the epitome of "the ambiguous hero" who signals a "triumph of interiorization."[18] According to Bazin, Bogart embodies qualities of decline as the actor "progressively wasted away" (99) in his films of the 1950s, where he appears with a chalky complexion, sunken cheeks, hollow yet still expressive eyes. In this visage, Bazin concludes, we "admire precisely the eminence and dignity of our decay" in the person of "this existentialist maturity which gradually transforms life into a stubborn irony at the expense of death" (99–101).

For all that, Bazin was far from the type of the figure of the Baudelairean modern, world-alienated and self-alienated, compulsively self-reflexive in the face of a degraded modernity. In its broad contours that was the model of his increasingly heretical novitiates, who explored cinema's modernism in something of the spirit in which Bazin explored its realism. Their work in criticism was largely complete on Bazin's passing—as legend has it, he died on the same day Francois Truffaut began shooting his first feature—but even under his tutelage they subsumed and superseded his credos, modifying or abandoning the precepts they inherited from him in light of their own concerns with the nature of film form, the functions of self-consciousness in cinematic expression, and perhaps above all the constitution of film authorship. Their fervent cinephilia remains in debt to Bazin, following him in viewing cinema at its best as a species of poetry. (It was Bazin, after all, who popularized the phrase "poetic realism" to describe French cinema of the 1930s and celebrated the poetry even of Italian Neo-Realism.) But Bazin's descendants embraced a more pessimistic existentialism, closer in mood to Camus's absurdism than Sartre's promotion of free will, and they revived the spirit of Surrealism that Bazin had left behind by the 1950s. By 1957, the work of Claude Lévi-Strauss had become a reference point in the pages of *Cahiers du Cinéma*, and the auteurists absorbed influences of structuralism not for its illustrations of the workings of myth, the strain that drew Bazin, but in its countervailing, demystifying vein, stressing the limits that prevailing structures place on possibilities of expression.

Among Jean-Luc Godard's early work in film criticism is an essay that stands as a systematic refutation of Bazinian aesthetics, even though Bazin is never mentioned there. In "Defense and Illustration of Classical Construction" (1952), he begins with a swipe at Sartre for imposing metaphysics on phenomena and for demanding fictional heroes who answer Sartre's own philosophical imperatives—premises he takes to be evidence of vanity. He prefers the modesty of filmmakers like Joseph L. Mankiewicz, Mark Robson, and Otto Preminger, and denies the Bazinian positions that "classical construction" (*découpage*, or classical continuity editing) gives way to depth-of-field in the 1940s, and that deep-focus photography realizes cinematic essence by permitting nature to abide on film without manipulation. The directors he cites continue to use classical construction, he claims, and it produces a kind of psychological realism that restores a plurality of interpretation that in fact, for him, long takes with deep-focus lack. In other words, Godard asserts the exact opposite of what Bazin claims—namely, that it is not the long take but *découpage* that heightens ambiguity, due to its greater rhetorical energy, because the shifting arrangements and scales of shots as well as the rhythms and intensities of edits amplify questions of meaning. The self-effacement of the director in Bazin's schema minimizes the operations of cinematic discourse that Godard foregrounds.

Godard's praise of the modest, *non*-metaphysical self-assertions of directors like Mankiewicz, Robson, Preminger, or Ida Lupino prefigures by three years the establishment of the *politique des auteurs*. Admirers of Godard's work may be surprised to find him defending "classical construction" and chastising long takes, since his films dismantle the former and make extensive use of the latter. In general, the auteurists regarded classicism and modernism as not just perfectly compatible but inevitably intertwined, a stance that goes some way toward revealing the revisionist tendencies of their modernism. What qualifies a filmmaker for designation as an auteur is precisely the extent of his (or in rare cases like Lupino, her) having been deemed "modern." Thus, Bergman's *Summer with Monika*, as Godard remarks, "brought to a peak that renaissance in modern cinema whose high priests were [Federico] Fellini in Italy, [Robert] Aldrich in Hollywood, and (so we believed, wrongly perhaps) Vadim in France."[19] Vadim, as it happened, had earlier been declared the only truly modern director in France, with the exclusionary cast of this proclamation underlining the sense in which the honorific "modern" was reserved for a select group of directors—mostly, the Hollywood auteurs. When Jacques Rivette announced in December 1955 that "the age of the auteurs is here at last" (95), he added that the small number then dubbed auteurs all had one thing in common, that they were "motivated by the same desire to produce work that is modern" (95).

What is it that makes this work "modern," especially as it stands in distinction to a vast body of work that evidently fails to achieve that standard? Rivette approaches direct answers in his piece on the "age of the auteur." There, he describes a sensibility that mingles self-consciousness with a kind of heightened naivety. Rivette refers to a pervasive sense of doom, of being near the end of things, that constitutes a particular consciousness of being modern and is shared among the auteurists' generation. It "pass[es] beyond the long period of submission to the manufactured product" (96) to "renew its links" with the origins of cinema and to express its own relation to that lineage. It marks a "return to lyricism, powerful feelings, melodrama," it rediscovers "a certain breadth of gesture, an externalizing of the roughest and most spontaneous emotions, in short, the rediscovery of naivety" (96). It gives an image of contemporary reality and marks a rupture with an older order. This is a version of modernism with commonalities to previous modernisms in the demand for self-reflection and the dictate to "make it new," although it embraces mass-cultural elements like melodrama that the "higher" modernisms repudiated— and indeed, Rivette wryly notes how art-cinema audiences sneer at the films of Nicholas Ray, who would become the most lauded of Hollywood auteurs among the *Cahiers* writers.

Such major modifications of modernist dogma were obviously necessary to locate any version at all of modernism in Hollywood, formerly held to be the ultimate haven of everything modernism had stood *against*. Obviously, the *Cahiers* writers detested what they called the "dictatorship of the producers"; their calls to renew the spirit of the silent era invoked in part the age of an industry not yet consolidated, before the tyranny of the script and the dominion of genre and narrative. By the 1950s, however, the auteurists took it for granted that Hollywood had indeed become fully institutionalized—though faced, significantly, with a loss of power and cultural authority—and the key to the *politique* is that it discovers vestiges of personal style within films that cannot avoid, in another sense, also being Hollywood product. It is the complex interaction of auteurs' "vision" with the standardized forms through which it gains expression that lends it the immediacy and spontaneity—and indeed, the naivety—that the auteurists glorify. The auteur may well still turn out to be a type of the romanticized individual genius— after one has registered the severity of restrictions on the means of communication, or acknowledged that the *Cahiers* writers paid as much attention to the dynamics of collaboration as most film critics had before them. (See, for example, Godard's remarks on the contributions of Bob Fosse's choreography and

Harry Stradling's cinematography to *The Pajama Game* [Stanley Donen, 1957], or his remarks on Reginald Rose's script for *Man of the West* [Anthony Mann, 1958].) Indeed, filmmakers like John Huston or Stanley Kubrick, who commanded a certain sporadic independence from the dictates of the studio system, were viewed with suspicion by the auteurists, found potentially guilty of an arrogant exceptionalism and therefore evincing naivety of a more vitiating kind. To be modern, after all, meant not to claim exemption from but to speak *through* the forms, structures, institutions, and systems that constitute and stratify modern reality, and to struggle with the problems of expression they incite.

The auteurist conception of modernism was neither fixed nor monolithic. In general, the *Cahiers* writers moved toward an understanding more in keeping with the main lines of modernist thought in the course of their work of the 1950s, culminating in Eric Rohmer's dramatic heralding of Alain Resnais's devoutly modernist *Hiroshima, Mon Amour* in 1959 as the first truly modern film of the sound cinema—as if to sweep the Hollywood auteurs aside in a single stroke just as the auteurists began their own film careers, in which they continued to explore ramifications of cinematic modernism. Godard also admired Resnais's overtly self-reflexive style: "[A] movement of the camera gives the impression that it was not simply a movement of the camera but an exploration of the secret of this movement."[20] His very next piece finds a similar effect in the decidedly more occulted stylistics of the Hollywood auteur Anthony Mann, whose *Man of the West*, says Godard, is "both course and discourse, or both beautiful landscapes and an explanation of this beauty."[21] This increasingly valorized self-reflexivity calls forth an ever greater awareness of problems intrinsic to acts of filming—especially after Godard began making films himself. Indeed, he reconsiders his admiration for Mankiewicz because *The Quiet American* (1958) exhibits too much intelligence, that is to say, too little awareness of the difficulties of its own enterprise, *too* mired, ultimately, in classical construction. He dubs short films "anti-cinema" because their brevity deprives them of an ability to question themselves. In other words, from his early defense of classical construction, Godard works his way toward a full-fledged modernism rooted in the problematics of cinematic textuality itself. The significance of modernism remains constant across auteurist writing, even if its definitions evolve differently for each of the *Cahiers* critics.

A fleeting essence: The *politique des auteurs* as film theory

If the auteurists were united around a set of ideas in progress, they were also engaged in expounding a kind of collective sensibility in critical practice, much as they would be in the following decade in their filmmaking practice. The range of styles across their films of the 1960s relates to whatever binding premises made the *nouvelle vague* a veritable "movement," at least in theory, in something of the same manner that the diversity of these writers' work yields to an overarching consonance, predicated on a particular *way* of thinking about cinema. Indeed, their individual differences as critics touchingly prefigure aspects of their work as filmmakers. As in his films, Godard is the most manic of the group, capable of shifting on a dime from vernacular to elevated registers, or of clearing a lump in his throat in honor of a film's pathos only to express some impulsive disdain in the next instant. Truffaut is the most pugnacious and the most generous by turns; Chabrol the most lucid and concrete, the most concerned with communicating interpretations of particular films. Rivette is the most aspirational, whose writing for all its magisterial turns most shows the strain of his convulsive efforts to come to terms with the challenges of individual works. Rohmer is the most theoretical, the most faithful disciple of Bazin, though often at war with his own didactic inclinations. Luc Moullet, a latecomer who joins the cabal as the decade wanes, adopts a tone of punk belligerence, as if to counter an air of intimidation in the company of his elders, foreshadowing the films he would begin to make in 1966, only after the *nouvelle vague* had already crested.

Yet for all its variety, the common ground among these writers is solid enough to certify their work as comprising a genre of sorts, roughly uniform in style and spirit. *Cahiers* writing overall is marked by a certain eccentricity, at least by comparison to prior writing on film in a journalistic mode. Not surprisingly, the *Cahiers* critics give no credence to the function of consumer advocacy that had justified for decades the role of the critic on the staff of many a newspaper or magazine, guiding the potential moviegoer with efficiently packaged information on available fare much as a more stalwart reporter might chronicle news of the day. Writing for a monthly periodical dedicated to a single subject, the *Cahiers* critics had the luxury of assuming an interested reader already familiar with films under discussion. Indeed, they often appear to be addressing one another, and one of the pleasures of reading their work is the sense it gives of eavesdropping on the dialogue among a sect of inspired apostles. By contrast to established practice, a typical *Cahiers* film review of this era pays only lip service to such staples of the form as plot and character, if it mentions them at all. A comparable publication like *Sight & Sound* in England appears positively stodgy in its quaint insistence on providing readers with synopses, cast listings, and other helpful tidbits. That journal took an obvious old-fashioned pride in its editorial responsibility entirely at odds with the insurgent streak of *Cahiers du Cinéma* in the years of the *politique*, fearlessly tendentious, playful, and casually provocative, keen to exclude any reader deemed insufficiently passionate about the cinema—with a capital C. All that the *Cahiers* critics take for granted is a gauge of their unapologetic address to an audience of cinephiles. They typically begin where previous film critics, with their breezy, once-over-lightly appraisals, left off. This is not to suggest that this body of writing lacks breeziness; the work is by turns gnomic, roguish, witty, given to cavalier gestures for all its ardent conviction. What concerns these critics, however, is less the vicissitudes of individual films than their relation to something insuperably larger. Once the *politique* was fully enshrined, its merriest slogan was "There are no works—only auteurs!" But on the evidence of their writing, even the greatest "masters" had to yield to the grandeur of that ultimate deity—the Cinema itself.

Crucial to the *Cahiers* method, and key to its breeziness, is the effort to convey in broad strokes the sense that any given film has received microscopic scrutiny. "Each shot of [Nicholas Ray's *Hot Blood*] proves ... that the director is not totally uninterested," writes Godard, with characteristic whimsy, while Rivette finds in the films of Howard Hawks that "each shot has a functional beauty" (128). "Every shot in the film is crowded with [Truffaut's] ideas and imagination" (53), Fereydoun Hoveyda avers of his colleague's first feature, *The 400 Blows* (1959). This implication that the film in question has been rigorously atomized down to its finest monad is somewhat offset by the wider scope of that "each" and "every." Indeed, the rhetoric of extremity—*always, never, only*—abounds in this work: "Hawksian drama is always expressed in spatial terms" (129), or again, "For Anthony Mann, landscape is always stripped of its dramatically picturesque effects" (167). The Italian Neo-Realists "have never compromised. Never" (36). Nicholas Ray, writes Truffaut, "[l]ike Rossellini ... never explains, he never emphasizes" (110). "Never before have characters been so close and yet so far away" (119), Godard observes of Ray's *Bitter Victory* (1957). Yet again: "In the arbitrary worlds of [André] Cayatte or [Henri-Georges] Clouzot ... only puppets can exist" (144). Or: "There's only one filmmaker left [in France] who hasn't sold out, and that's [Robert] Bresson," Rivette declaims in a 1957 editorial roundtable, adding for good measure, "He's the only one" (36).

These tendencies define the vertiginous range of *Cahiers* writing from the molecular to the cosmic, a spectrum commonly traversed in a trice, often in a single line, in leaps of logic by turns mystifying and exhilarating. As a matter of idiosyncratic routine, the *Cahiers* critics convey the impression that they have conducted extremely close readings of the films they review, yet they paraphrase these minute analyses in the most sweeping terms. Even so, these broad exegeses are liberally punctuated by vivid, glancing evocations of illustrative instants, heightened moments, passing details. Godard's review of Samuel Fuller's *Forty Guns* (1957) exemplifies the approach; in this piece, Godard starts with a feverish tribute to Fuller's seemingly modest B-movie, proclaiming that each scene and every shot is "so rich in invention ... so bursting with daring conceptions" that it is redolent of "the extravagances of Abel Gance and Stroheim, or purely and simply of Murnau."[22] He goes on to describe in antic detail three discrete moments from the film, entirely without context, the best scene lasting only three seconds. The tone is comic, as the writer calls characters by the names of the actors playing them, using the actors' first names in a jesting show of mock-familiarity. Even if this tone qualifies the high praise somewhat, the review aptly illustrates the *Cahiers* writers' penchant for seizing upon the passing glance, the fleeting moment.

There is a struck-by-lightning quality about the auteurists' apprehension of these cinematic flashes that has everything to do with their notion of the auteur. In one sense, the auteur is posited as an oracular figure who stands as a medium between the individual work and the Cinema itself. He differs from a director who is *not* an auteur—that is to say, almost all of them—in the capacity to conduct the electrical charge exchanged from the one to the other. The auteur's "mastery" (if any) resides in channeling the energies of the cosmic through the molecular in these exalted moments, with the *Cahiers* critics narrating the effort as an epic struggle, noble in itself, yet seemingly doomed to a failure made great by the adversity that predestines it. Indeed, if the auteurists romanticize anything, it is this very failure. The best case in point is their treatment of an auteur like Nicholas Ray, who was without peer in the front rank of their emerging pantheon, as the flaws of Ray's films figure prominently in their celebration of his achievement. From *On Dangerous Ground* (1951) through *Hot Blood* (1958), the *Cahiers* critics trace Ray's travails within the studio system—the "kingdom of mechanization" (105)—as Ray crafts "small objects out of holly wood" (108), in Truffaut's words, and "loses the battle even before he starts fighting" (108). In the films themselves, the auteurists variously discover indifference and clumsiness, finding in *Rebel Without a Cause*, for example, too much naïve psychoanalysis of the characters. Truffaut delivers the unadorned verdict that "[a]ll his films are very disjointed," he "is not of great stature as a technician," and "[t]he editing of [*Johnny Guitar* (1954)] is deplorable" (108). Writing on *Hot Blood*, Godard declares that the plot is "badly handled" (117) and that the film as a whole is "anodyne" (108). With all this going against him, Ray is lucky indeed to enjoy, in Rivette's words, "the most constant privilege of the masters," that of "seeing everything, including the most simple mistakes, tend to their advantage rather than diminishing their stature" (104).

Even so, it is a curious form of idolatry that fixes so resolutely upon the debilities of the worshipped. How are these clear-eyed negative judgments compatible at all with a rendition of Ray as a "master"? In one sense, this is the essential question of auteurism. The *Cahiers* critics are keenly aware of cutting against the grain of prevailing opinion; nearly every time they write about Ray in the 1950s, they note a dominant critical consensus against him. Rivette concedes that readers are likely to be "surprised" to see him give Ray the benefit of the doubt in reviewing an apparently inferior film, but he bluntly rejoins that, in that case, "you are ill-prepared to appreciate" (104) such a film. In his piece on *Hot Blood*, Godard remarks, "I can hear people saying, it is just a commercial chore about gipsies [*sic*]"—and he coolly grants that such dissenters may well be right before lurching into this thicket of epigrams:

> A success almost in spite of its director, I should add; or better, brought off by Nicholas Ray's innate sense of cinema; in an automatic manner, therefore, but less naively than that

writing beloved of the early surrealists. The whole cinema
and nothing but the cinema, I was saying of Nicholas Ray.
This eulogy entails a reservation. Nothing but cinema may
not be the whole cinema. (117)

The maneuver is clearly intended to place such objections
entirely beside the point.

Godard maintained a part-time vocation as a put-on artist
throughout his career, and the intonations of that attitude
are certainly audible here. The more ardent tones of *Cahiers*
writing often betray a countercurrent of self-deflation, a point
not unrelated to the habit of elevating auteurs by virtue of
their failings rather than simply in spite of them. Twenty years
later, in the thick of his career as a filmmaker, Rohmer returned
to criticism to salute the last film of another auteurist "master,"
Jean Renoir. In his tribute to *The Little Theater of Jean Renoir*
(1970), Rohmer pinpoints what he deems the awkwardness of
Renoir's methods before concluding that the film stands as an
emblem of film art for future generations because it "contains
all of cinema."[23] Godard's rhetorical flourish is coy while
Rohmer's is manifestly sincere; what they have in common
is a kind of blithe holism, capable of seeing worlds in grains
of sand or in finding "all of cinema" in a single film or an
adventitious detail—and a film scaled disproportionately at
that, in this case, at least in the sense of its consisting of a series
of sketches produced for television.

When Godard cautions that "nothing but cinema may not
be the whole cinema," the witty conceit of his aphorism recalls
the legalistic phrase "nothing but the truth" and thus prefigures
the famous Godardian proclamation that the "cinema is truth
twenty-four times per second." Both epigrams characterize
auteurist writing in the sense that the *Cahiers* critics routinely
ascribe attributes of will to "the cinema" as such, granting
it kinds of volition as a medium denied to even the greatest
of auteurs, like Renoir or Ray. That the cinema equals truth
stands, in this declaration, as a precept independent of specific
practitioners, whether auteurs, auteurists, or mere directors. At

the end of the piece on *Hot Blood*, Godard seems to be saying that Ray is forced back on his "innate" feeling for the cinema by the deficiencies of material that cannot be fully redeemed even by this "pure" strain ("nothing but the cinema").

In the same piece, as cited above, Godard invokes the Surrealists explicitly to comment on the nature of Ray's authorship. "Automatic writing" was understood as inscription derived from an unknown or even mystic source, as if produced by language itself, a notion embraced by the Surrealists as a means to tap the unconscious. Godard's direct reference to automatic writing renders such standard questions of authorship as intention or consciousness essentially moot, positioning the auteur as a kind of astral body *without* conscious will, a divining rod between some ideal manifestation of the Cinema and an ephemeral material embodiment providing at best only glimpses of the glorified paradigm.

The Surrealist fascination with cinema was rooted in similar notions. For the Surrealists, the cinema was understood as an "automatic" medium that could, in the course of its operations, reflect in some mysterious and complicated way the human interventions that set the machinery in motion. Yet the machinery had a life of its own to be explored rather than repressed, as in the reverse-motion or slow-motion effects common in Surrealist films from Germaine Dulac's *The Seashell and the Clergyman* (1928) to Jean Cocteau's *Blood of a Poet* (1931) or Jean Vigo's *Zero for Conduct* (1934). It is against this background that Jean Epstein articulated the notion of *photogénie*, naming a unit of cinematic being, a monad, a moment, simply the "photogenic" in literal terms, that which lends itself to being filmed, but really the glimpse that lays bare in an instant some passing cinematic essence, not transcending the mechanism of the form but disclosing a real presence that leaps up at intervals alongside it—and of course, at other intervals when the machinery takes over, disappears.

The legacy of Surrealism and these ideas in particular inform auteurism at virtually every level. Among other things, the notion of *photogénie* implies an affinity between cinema and poetry, and Surrealist experiments in film are largely devoted to exploring this nexus, animating the medium's lyric potential by harnessing its automatism, working with non-narrative forms, using techniques of associative editing, orchestrating dreamlike structures. Similarly, though the auteurists attend in the 1950s predominantly to commercial narrative films, neglecting experimental cinemas of all kinds, they tend to emphasize their nonnarrative qualities and declare a spirit of experimentation to be a key measure of value. Of Charles Laughton's *The Night of the Hunter* (1955), for example, Truffaut writes that it "makes us fall in love again with an experimental cinema that truly *experiments*."[24] Ray's career culminated in a remarkable excursion into experimental film, *We Can't Go Home Again* (1973/2009), but the auteurists were already hailing him as a quasi-avant-gardist during his years in the studio system. How could Ray still be the quintessential auteur when his work was declared so roundly deficient by the very critics who celebrated him? The answer is that those deficiencies were faults only by standards very different from the ones the celebrants applied. The standards that led establishment critics to dismiss Nicholas Ray as an amateur are precisely the standards the auteurists rejected, based on a model of cinema as essentially narrative and allied with the craftily plotted tale, the classical realist novel, the well-made play. The auteurist model was essentially *anti*narrative, defined by the lyric strophe, the poetic intuition, the soaring crescendo or the dying fall, the rhythmic creation of beauty.

Hence the construction of the auteur as cinematic poet, with Ray as the paragon. Ray "is a poet, of that there is no doubt" (113), Rohmer states flatly, while Truffaut adds, "He is the poet of nightfall" (108). According to Rivette, Ray finds beauty in "a circuitous dilation of expressive detail," "a certain breadth of modern gesture," a "taste for paroxysm" (105). The bold uses of color, the arrangement of figures in the frame, the fiercely asymmetrical widescreen compositions in their fugitive relation to more conventionally balanced ones—these formal dimensions are the aspects of Ray's work that the *Cahiers* critics turned to, after serenely accepting their adversaries' imputations of weak plotting or naïve psychology—then categorically declaring the cinema off limits to these same opponents. Yet the auteurist poetry of the cinema is of a special kind, not only in its tendency to flare up at intervals in texts that are not, in any ordinary sense, poems. In fact, it is a species of poetry that could *only* occur in such contexts; its very existence depends on its being contained within more prosaic structures, and its emanations exhilarate the auteurists precisely in the way that it breaches and disrupts those more stable forms.

Glimmerings of essentialism certainly flicker in auteurists' eyes, but it is considerably mitigated by the *Cahiers* critics' intense responsiveness to conditions of Hollywood in the 1950s. In its earliest formulations, the *politique des auteurs* extends editorial support to a small number of Hollywood directors—namely, as of 1955, four: Robert Aldrich, Richard Brooks, Anthony Mann, and Nicholas Ray. All four emerged after the Second World War and achieved prominence in the following decade as Hollywood underwent a series of setbacks, from the "Paramount" Decree that challenged the studios' monopolistic practices to the House Un-American Activities Committee's investigations and the irrevocable loss of a large share of the mass audience to competition from television. These circumstances are cited only in passing by the *Cahiers* critics, but their effects pervade auteurist writing. Their work of the 1950s expresses a strong impression of a powerful institution in crisis, with the auteurs as harbingers of its waning days who might also, in this period of volatile transition, transform it altogether. In the first of his essays to use the word "auteur" in its emerging sense, Rivette celebrates the "violence" of the four auteurs named above as "a weapon" that is "the external sign of rupture" recalling the "*coup d'état*" of Orson Welles in the 1940s that had already "cracked to its very foundation the whole edifice of Hollywood production" (95). For the *Cahiers* writers, the auteurs were the antagonists abiding in the wake of this rupture, couriers of a new cinema, still beholden to the institution's authority, but exploiting its resources while heralding its decline.

The quartet of Aldrich, Brooks, Mann, and Ray certifies the commitment to youth culture that undergirded the *politique des auteurs*, but even in relation to the work of this favored four, the *Cahiers* writers revert constantly to tropes of defeat and perishability—as suggested in Godard's characterization of his own piece on *Hot Blood* as a "eulogy," with connotations of funereal oration. The policy quickly extended to include directors whose earliest work dated to the silent era, like Ford, Hawks, Hitchcock, Lang, McCarey, Sternberg, Stroheim, or Raoul Walsh, or to the first generation of sound, like Preminger or Welles, as well as a cadre of art-cinema filmmakers from Murnau to Bresson. The work of the younger auteurs is typically celebrated for its glimmerings of improbable brilliance wrested from among the oddments of a moribund industry. Writing on the older auteurs, meanwhile, the *Cahiers* critics are ever aware of their age and of the rich, mottled histories they trundle behind them. In either case, auteurism arises as an elegiac reaction to perceived lateness, a stringent tribute to the cinema and its "masters" in the era of their decline, undertaken with equal parts of exuberance and melancholy.

The auteurist treatment of Fritz Lang's work of the 1950s is perhaps the most telling case in this regard. Lang's move from Germany to Hollywood in the 1930s was widely viewed as a fall from grace in itself in the career of this crucial director, but many films from the first years of his expatriation garnered critical adulation, including *You Only Live Once* (1937) and *Woman in the Window* (1944). By the 1950s, Lang had fallen out of favor with studios like Twentieth Century Fox and was under a cloud of suspicion with the HUAC, due more to his status as an émigré than to any political expression or activity. Consequently, many of the projects of this final decade of his career, however distinguished, have a somewhat cobbled-together quality, their critical receptions ranging from lukewarm to distinctly hostile, with a few key exceptions like *The Big Heat*.

Lang's last Hollywood film, *Beyond a Reasonable Doubt* (1956), is often cited as his worst, including by the director himself. Rivette's review in *Cahiers du Cinéma* approached it with the odd kind of reverence that typifies auteurist practice, dismissing severely, one by one, the objections of unknown traducers. At the core of the film Rivette sees "a proliferation of denials" (140), a series of gestures against ordinary cinematic pleasures. It is, he says, "the absolute antithesis of 'an entertaining evening'" (141). Indeed, the film Rivette describes is one leached of energy, inert, "diagrammatic" (140), its materials treated as so much "data" (141). The willful contrivance of a plot twist—in which the main character, a reporter who gets himself convicted of murder to expose liabilities of capital punishment, proves to be *actually* guilty—is treated by Rivette as evidence of the film's "conceptual" character, a "dialectical inversion" (141) revealing a drive to internal coherence that fulfills aspirations traceable, Rivette insists, to Lang's earliest work to construct "a *totally closed* world" (141, emphasis in original). In keeping with auteurist protocols, Rivette reads the film through Lang's work as a whole, discovering in turn a dialectical relation to the director's oeuvre: "In the earlier films, innocence with all the appearance of guilt; here, guilt with all the appearance of innocence" (143). The formulation is typical in its aphoristic crispness but a bit too neat to hold; for all its aplomb, the single example of *M.* (1931) is enough to call it into question.

As so often in auteurist practice, Rivette thus finds greatness of a sort in the very qualities a film's detractors derided—in the case of the Lang, its blankness, its starkness, the torpid, mechanical character of its execution. Overall, the auteurist model of commitment to cinema has a crucial dimension of the penitential, calling upon adherents to submit themselves to varieties of *un*-pleasure from excruciation to aesthetic inertia. Ultimately, Rivette reads *Beyond a Reasonable Doubt* as a magisterial expression of disdain for prevailing models of cinematic pleasure, insulating itself from that petty province by building a "*totally closed* world" out of its materials—

miraculously enough, considering the sparseness of its means. Indeed, much of the critical consensus on Lang in the 1950s was conditioned by a perception of indignity, that the once-powerful director had sunk to Poverty Row—never more than with *Beyond a Reasonable Doubt*, produced by a penny-pinching independent (Bert E. Friedlob). Along with most of the *Cahiers* writers, Rivette valued on principle "low-budget" filmmaking over so-called quality productions with a prefabricated studio polish. On a parallel track with the development of auteurism, Rivette in particular deconstructed traditional cinematic economies, demystifying lavishness and celebrating the ingenuity of filmmakers in overcoming reduced circumstances with cinematic invention—not just in the case of Lang but in those of Preminger, Welles, and the Italian Neo-Realists. Reconceiving signifiers of impoverishment as potential sites of bounty, Rivette pursues a "eulogy to poverty" persistently across his work of the 1950s, with the recurrence of that word "eulogy" suggesting the element of mortification within this penitential streak of auteurism.

The *politique des auteurs* was a project of trans-valuation dedicated, among other things, to overturning the critical establishment's general preferences for refined, tasteful, polished, respectably packaged cinema. To convert the putatively indigent look of "low-budget" filmmaking into a virtual badge of honor—a mark of unpretentiousness if not sheer beauty, even of spiritual purity, instead of a shameful lack—was an important step, with the implication that a film's surface appearance might bely its occulted value, or be belied by it. As a key part of this project, the *Cahiers* writers tirelessly defended a series of films through the 1950s and 1960s generally regarded as "failed" work—from Welles's *Mr. Arkadin* (1955) through late works of Chaplin and Renoir to Dreyer's *Gertrud* (1964) or Hitchcock's *Marnie* (1964). In these crucial cases and many others, the auteurists boldly proclaimed the unequivocal value—indeed, the greatness—of films declared beyond the pale by prevailing critical opinion. *Mr. Arkadin* was so derided that it did not premiere in the United States, its director's native country, until 1962, seven years after its European release, when it was greeted with vitriolic reviews. Meanwhile, four years earlier, it had bowed as number six on the *Cahiers* list of the greatest films of all time. Another key auteur, Howard Hawks, enjoyed more consistent industry support in the 1950s than either Lang or Welles, but he too dabbled in the B-movie (with *The Thing* [1951]) and found his work increasingly denigrated, as the studio system went into decline, by comparison with his films of the golden age. Rivette begins a 1953 piece on "The Genius of Howard Hawks" with the observation that although Hawks's brilliance should be self-evident upon viewing the films, "some people don't admit this" and "refuse to be satisfied by truth" (126). The against-the-grain tendency of Rivette's analysis is clear from the start, as he emphasizes the tragic overtones of Hawksian comedy, viewing Hawks's films as "parables of ruin" preoccupied—albeit lyrically—with "ugliness and foulness" and expressing a "fascination" with "infantilism, degradation, or decadence" (127). As in the *Cahiers* treatment of most auteurs, Rivette remarks matter-of-factly on an enfeebled quality of the work, noting in Hawks's case a certain "monotony" and "lassitude" about the films. But these seeming liabilities are turned again to the auteur's advantage once referred to larger structural principles and an overall mood or climate of the auteur's work as a whole. That "monotony," as it turns out, is "only a façade" (129), for example, while the "lassitude" turns out to be a "dramatic device" (129) deployed to remarkable effect. Though Rivette concludes by allowing that Hawks's work may ultimately be an "affirmation" of sorts, he poses along the way a rhetorical question with considerable mitigating force: "Could we be offered a more bitter view of life than this?" (126). One may have to remind oneself that the film that occasions these reflections is none other than *Monkey Business* (1952)—a whimsical light comedy viewed on its release by American critics as a frivolous and failed effort to recapture the spirit of Hawks's earlier screwball comedies like *Bringing Up Baby* (1938).

In its earliest forms, auteurist critical practice thrives on façades and false appearances, forever exposing a core of value that is dazzlingly self-evident despite being invisible to oblivious others, a core that, once disclosed, renders even that seemingly unlovely surface a thing of beauty. The blithe acknowledgment of a given auteur's faults serves to clear the way for the revelation to come. In one of the earliest and most telling *Cahiers* accounts of American cinema, "Rediscovering America" (1955)—a sequel of sorts, one year later, to Truffaut's "Certain Tendency of the French Cinema"—Rohmer traces his conversion from mistrust of that cinema to a passionate embrace of its achievements and possibilities, especially by contrast with the "perpetual drivel" (91) of French cinema. The primal scene of this change of heart is a screening of Frank Capra's *It Happened One Night* (1934), at which "the cinema held up to me … a face without artifice, unpolished but not rough" (88). Such epiphanic experience—in the sense of *seeing through* to an inner manifestation—pervades auteurist writing of the 1950s, as the *Cahiers* critics strive convulsively to express, at once, the sudden, transitory, and processual dimensions of their viewing experiences. Auteurist writing commonly describes specific showings of films in a spirit of speculative reverie, parsing evolving responses to films as they unfold, or across successive screenings. Claude Chabrol's review of Hitchcock's *Rear Window* (1954), for example, recounts a deeper sense of the film on a subsequent encounter that "make[s] it possible to brush aside the objections and the criticisms that ensued after a superficial viewing" (136) earlier, even in the face of "the piteous blindness of the skeptics" (139). A repeated move from a rhetorical skepticism to an ardent faith typifies the *Cahiers* style in this period, with the writer often sketching a personal trajectory from an initial blindness to an ultimate insight. Rivette's piece on *Beyond a Reasonable Doubt*, for instance, traces phases of response to the film from a bemused first impression of emptiness and schematism to increasing fascination, with the growing inclination to "suppose this to be some stratagem, and wait and see what happens" (140).

In one of his final contributions to *Cahiers du Cinéma*, in 1957, Bazin himself weighed in on the *politique des auteurs*, fully accepting the premise that "when one is dealing with genius, it is always a good method to presuppose that a supposed weakness in a work of art is nothing other than a beauty that one has not yet managed to understand" (256). Even so, Bazin inveighs against the excesses of his younger colleagues, albeit in a spirit of patrician indulgence, in terms that would become increasingly familiar as auteurism waned in the 1960s at *Cahiers* while spreading to England, the United States, and elsewhere. He chides auteurist propensities to accord too much importance to B-films, to "read in" tendentious meanings to films of slight significance, and to promote directors' lesser works simply because they happen to come later in a given auteur's career, citing *Mr. Arkadin* as the chief example of this penchant. Bazin grants that *Citizen Kane* "cannot help remaining to a certain extent an RKO product" and that *Arkadin* has "more of Orson Welles in it" (255).

Yet the cult of personality that auteurism potentially enables, in Bazin's view, denies the manifold contingencies that present constant predicaments to filmmakers, as well as the myriad social determinants that condition individuals. According to Bazin, in a famous formulation, the American cinema is to be admired "not only for the talent of this or that filmmaker, but the genius of the system, the richness of its ever-vigorous tradition, and its fertility when it comes into contact with new elements" (258). By auteurist standards this estimation could only have seemed naively idealistic. Even though Bazin acknowledges that restrictions on production were heavier in Hollywood than elsewhere, this "genius of the system" apparently guaranteed a compensatory fertility—a qualification the auteurists would surely never have granted. While Bazin selectively supports certain auteurist propositions—and was himself the author of one of the first critical monographs on a film director with his 1950 book on Orson Welles—he misses the grand ambition to alter fundamentally basic criteria of cinematic value.

In any case, Bazin is obviously right to cite *Mr. Arkadin* as a crucial test case. Rohmer wrote a long piece on the film, and for the rest (extrapolation being such a crucial part of the method) it is easy enough to infer the more general quality of auteurist esteem for this film from the known values in abundant supply in the rest of their work. A sort of shoestring deconstruction of *Citizen Kane, Mr. Arkadin* concerns a roguish arriviste's investigation into the past of a supposedly amnesiac magnate, a quest commissioned by the grandee himself. A hectic catalog of the techniques Welles had pieced together to form his personal signatures—long takes, deep-focus cinematography, erratically or elegantly mobile framing (and sometimes both at once), extreme camera angles, fractured narratives, expressionistic light design and layered sound design—the film illustrates the heady patchwork quality of Welles's "late" work (at the ripe old age of thirty-nine), and the bracing independence of these signatures from the buttresses of studio technology. Though *Mr. Arkadin* retains fragments of vagrant genres (film noir, Cold War thriller, "great man" pseudo-biopic in the manner of *Citizen Kane*) and other residues of popular narrative forms, it lays the groundwork for the new kinds of filmmaking practice that Welles would restlessly explore for the next three decades, even more remote from standard industry models—and providing one of the clearest templates for the earliest films the auteurists would go on to make as pioneers of the *nouvelle vague*.

The *Cahiers* critics were most responsive to a particular *rhythm* they identified in the films of Hollywood auteurs, produced by an interweaving of the conventional matter of "the system" and the bolts of inspiration loosed by the auteur's inventive antagonism. Thus Rivette speaks of a "banal character" in Preminger's work that is also "fresh and surprising," and of the tonic effect of "the alternation of successful passages with others of unruffled awkwardness" (133). In the piece on *Rear Window*, Chabrol refers even more explicitly to the distinctive "rhythm of the work," stoked by a blend of elements defined as "clumsy" and "naïve," with the "inexpressible poetry" that inexorably creeps into the otherwise "stifling atmosphere"(138–139) of the film. Though the auteurists surely celebrated the post-studio ambience of *Mr. Arkadin*, they must have reveled as well in its ragged, episodic structure and its jolting, irregular textures ("unpolished but not rough"). Even if Welles was freed from the oppression of Hollywood in his late work, no auteur could believe himself to be ultimately liberated, if only because he remained inevitably in thrall to himself. Indeed, in a film like *Mr. Arkadin*, Welles could easily have been consigned to a kind of default amateur status that set his cinematic inventiveness into stark relief— like Preminger, whose affinity with the "amateur," according to Rivette, "reduces his art to the essential" (132). Moreover, in his exile from the studio system, Welles remained a nominally abject figure, thus fulfilling the common stipulation of the auteur as existentialist antihero. Bazin's critique of the *politique des auteurs* formulates the policy more explicitly than any of its practitioners ever deigned to do. Earlier, Rohmer quipped that Truffaut had offered for a while to define it but "what is already well conceived need not be articulated."[25] That jovial abdication accounts in part for the simplified versions of "auteur theory" that make their way into English in the early 1960s under the banner of a hardy corps of masterful visionaries in unwavering possession of original, powerful, and coherent worldviews. Even if the figure of the auteur in *Cahiers* writing does maintain a certain consistency, unity and coherence are just about the *last* aesthetic values the auteurists espoused. It cannot really even be said that an auteur is simply a maker of great films, since so many auteurs' productions, as whole films, are approached with such ambivalence by the *Cahiers* writers.

For all the auteurists' passionate advocacy, few films even by auteurs are ever praised for their "unity"; so much at odds with the aesthetic was any such criterion that the auteurists hardly bother to polemicize against it, with rare exceptions like Godard's caveat taking issue with one critic's emphasis on unity to such an extent that every other aspect of a work is eclipsed. (The critic in question happened to be Alexandre Astruc, but that is another matter.) Elsewhere, Rivette speaks of a preferred model of film editing—namely montage—as "rediscovering unity from a basis in fragmentation, but without concealing the fragmentation in doing so; on the contrary, emphasizing it" (60–61). In what may be the most direct definition in auteurist writing of that vexed and crucial term mise-en-scène, Rivette states that it is "the relation of a precise complex of sets and characters, a network of relationships, an architecture of connections, an animated complex that seems suspended in space" (134). This notion of the film as a complex also comes closest to encapsulating the auteurist conception of cinematic form, implying a preference amply borne out in their cinematic practices for textual complications, unresolved elements, multifarious registers, and levels of meaning—far from the tasteful, entombed "unity" of, say, a literary adaptation by a "quality" director like Jean Aurenche. Indeed, the auteur's personal expression furnishes the most robustly energized nodes in this "network of relations," especially in its conflicted, dynamic interaction with so many other variables.

The *Cahiers* writers were drawn to contradiction and disruption above all. As Rohmer would have it, "Cinema's true nature is contradictory; one can enter its temple only by the door of paradox."[26] However, they granted the concept of "unity" a greater credence in existentialist terms, especially where auteurs were concerned. In Howard Hawks's films, according to Rivette, the "strength of the hero's will-power is an assurance of the man and the spirit, tied together on behalf of that which justifies their existence and gives it the highest meaning" (231). At least one critic takes this kind of rhetoric to be definitive: "An auteur was a film director who expressed an optimistic image of human potentialities within an utterly corrupt society. By reaching out emotionally and spiritually to other human beings and to God, one could transcend the isolation imposed on one by a corrupt world."[27] Such language certainly recurs in auteurist writing, but if we recall that Rivette's remarks encompass, in the very same article, Hawks's fascination with decadence and degradation, at least the "optimistic" element of this characterization seems in need of qualification. As Jim Hillier notes, Rivette was actually the least inclined to this kind of thinking among the auteurists; according to Hillier, it is Rohmer who "emphasizes universal themes" like will and destiny and "a certain idea of man," while Rivette's "'revolutionary' cinema stresses the desire of auteurs to produce work that is modern" (74). Yet even Rohmer foregrounds, precisely, the *bitterness* of Nicholas Ray's modernity; the "apathetic, petitbourgeois juveniles" of *Rebel*, he says, are "marked with the seal of the same fate" (112) as all his characters. However, the "modern image of fate is no banal, stupid accident … It is the disproportion that exists between the measure of man—always a noble one—and the futility of the task he often sets himself" (114–115). It is, Rohmer goes on, for politicians and philosophers "to show mankind horizons which are clearer than the ones it has chosen, but it is the poet's mission to doubt that optimism" (115)— and Nicholas Ray, as we first learned from the auteurists, was nothing if not a poet.

What qualities *were* common among the films and auteurs that the *Cahiers* writers championed? A streak of romantic-ironic fatalism was surely part of the mix, though a mordant indifference often attends their treatment of themes. Godard typically refers to themes like morality and liberty with an offhanded rhetoric, the verbal equivalent of a shrug, suggesting that when it came to the Big Ideas, any one could be as good as any other. The movies the auteurists loved the most split the difference between a tragic sense of life and an antic, even awkward, sense of the absurd. Lack of pretension was almost always lauded, as were—to cite a few words that recur most often across their work—qualities of "delirium," "lyricism," "starkness," "geometry" or a "geometrical" cast, "simplicity," "complexity," and "abstraction." The last is a word they often use with negative connotations, but which can also connote, in other contexts, the highest praise, surfacing at times to guard against clear liabilities like literal-mindedness. Despite the auteurist impatience with "important" themes—or more precisely, with films that treat themes with an air of *self*-importance—their favored cinema was, in fact, a cinema of ideas, albeit in a special and illuminating sense.

For the auteurists, ideas were not at all theses in the sense of, say, the so-called novel of ideas. That was what ideas meant in the despised Tradition of Quality, and the *Cahiers* writers were as keen to redefine the word for their purposes as they were to subvert that tradition. In general, for them, ideas were aesthetic, amounting to a kind of formal invention, as in Truffaut's gloss on the work of Robert Aldrich: " ... [I]t is not unusual to encounter a new idea with each shot. In [*Kiss Me Deadly* (1955)] the inventiveness is so rich that we don't know what to look at."[28] Ideas align with "precise details," with "an abstract, almost fairy-tale aspect" (95). A simple choice of camera angle could count as an idea so long as it had a "precise" or "original" relation to its material. The "abstract" aspect here is formal, not conceptual, as ideas work to counter or concretize general premises. As Godard remarks on Nicholas Ray's visual compositions, they "somehow manage to make ideas as abstract as Liberty and Destiny both clear and tangible."[29] On the one hand, according to Godard, Roger Vadim's mise-en-scéne is "a simple matter of logic" (49); on the other, it is his handling of ideas that qualifies him as the only modern director in France—a verdict Godard would later modify considerably: "Vadim will become a great director," Godard predicts in 1957, "because his scenes are never occasioned by a purely abstract or theoretical idea for a shot; rather, it is *the idea of a scene*, in other words, a dramatic idea, which occasions the *idea of a shot*" (49, emphasis in original). In their book on Hitchcock, Chabrol and Rohmer declare Hitchcock a director of ideas in the auteurist sense of the word, not because of the Catholic themes or premises about shared or transferred guilt they ascribe to him. Rather, ideas are located in visual realizations of material, in specific executions of shots and scenes. Thus, at the conclusion of *The*

Thirty-nine Steps (1935), the death of Mr. Memory discloses immanent meanings in concrete constructions, showing the "mechanism of confession and how it works" and formally realizing "a number of ideas that are dear to [Hitchcock]."[30]

Similarly, comparing Eisenstein and Welles in his review of *Mr. Arkadin*, Rohmer finds that "thanks to implicit or explicit *attractions*, we find the same ability to express more than a sentiment, to express an *idea*."[31] Rohmer co-opts the word "attractions" from Eisenstein himself, who used it to refer to a certain logic of film editing—to suggest the way in which even seemingly unrelated shots may appear dynamically "attracted" to one another in the movement from shot to shot—and to evoke the voluptuous, carnivalesque milieu of sideshow attractions. An attraction, says Eisenstein, is any element of the spectacle with an impact, calculated to produce certain emotional "shocks." By this definition, ideas seem to be something like the *opposite* of what they are commonly held to be—not propositions or concepts, academic or intellectual generalities conducive to reflection, but *sensory* units, jolting, kinetic, *exciting*.

Those sensations were the ones the auteurists sought most vitally, and in their work "ideas" serve as the mechanism of transmission, the crucial vehicle for the transference of feeling from auteur to spectator *through* the text. Never preoccupied with dithering about auteurs' intentions, the *Cahiers* writers seized upon felt intensities as varieties of expression. Their notion of the idea circumvents the usual questions of authorial intention since the "idea" is ultimately a point of charged correspondence between the semblance of creative consciousness and the kinetics of cinema itself. In 1950s auteurism, the spectator is granted far more agency than has usually been acknowledged—so much so that this work could easily be seen as model for conceiving the critic-as-artist, or a precursor of 1970s and 1980s-style reception theory, with its claims on behalf of the authority of the reader. As Rivette puts it, "It is up to the spectator to assume responsibility not only for thoughts and 'motives' of the characters ... it is up to him [*sic*] to know how to transform [the film's] contradictory moments" (142). The auteur may be the forger of the concept but the auteurist/spectator is its discoverer. Is a striking gesture by, say, Jean Simmons in *Angel Face* really an "idea" of the film's director, Otto Preminger? A staunch auteurist would scoff at the question, because the real point is less to credit creators than to convert gestures into "ideas" along with shots, cuts, objects, facial expressions, movements of limbs, bodily postures, turns of the camera, virtually all the materials of cinema including those of its own transmission—and thereby multiply possibilities for encountering cinematic elements as repositories of meaning.

Perhaps above all, the auteurists' cinema is one of exploration and discovery. But unlike Bazin's nature-centered version—as, for example, in his essay "Cinema and Exploration" (1949)—theirs is a *human*-centered cinema in which the auteur emerges as a cognate subject which channels the energies of cinema into communications of a force and intimacy that is sometimes startling, especially considering the remoteness the auteur maintains as an actual person. Auteurist reading is (at least) double-focused, with one eye on auteurs' signatures and another on the impersonal cinematic surround. The latter often excites the *Cahiers* critics as much as the former, though the occasions when the two strains coalesce provide their most sublime moments. With a helping hand from auteurs, it is in the power of cinema itself to intercept life, to excavate "hidden treasures everywhere" (90), to expose a "long-hidden grandeur" (130) of things, to seize possession, like Welles's Mr. Arkadin himself, "of the most modern power: the ability to move around, to be somehow present at the same moment all over the world."[32] This is a cinema of articulate kinesis, translating movement into terms dazzlingly specific to the medium and generating explosive excitements in these now-familiar yet still ineffable reconfigurations. These intensities are only amplified by the ways they spring up suddenly and pass inevitably. For the *Cahiers* writers, the ultimate paradox of this quintessentially paradoxical medium is its seemingly endless capacity to disclose the "fleeting essence" of matter or being. Yet, though it was these flashing, transient revelations they longed for the most, virtually every line they wrote attests to their recognition that an essence that flees—since the very concept requires changelessness—is really no essence at all.

"Auteur theory" in America

The American film critic Andrew Sarris is so closely identified with the conversion of the *politique des auteurs* into the "auteur theory" that it is striking to note, on reviewing his work, how little of it is devoted to the subject. Three essays make up the bulk of his contribution, extended in *The American Cinema*, an encyclopedia of sorts that has been called the bible of auteurism, with lively entries on dozens of directors who worked in Hollywood, ranked in standing according to broad categories from the "Pantheon Directors" at the apex to the "Lightly Likeable" or "Less than Meets the Eye" further down the line. The introduction of his first collection of film reviews, *Confessions of a Cultist*, goes out of its way to avoid using the word "auteur," even as it traces the process by which he embraced auteur theory as a critical method. Though the book's title reifies the method (while wittily embracing accusations of cultism by his critics) the closest he comes to acknowledging his association with auteurism is an arch, veiled reference to Pauline Kael's notorious polemic against auteur theory, and against Sarris himself. Later in the book, he brashly announces in a whimsical interview with himself that he doesn't care if his devaluation of certain directors (Delmer Daves and Jean Negulesco) sounds like a breach of auteur theory.

Though Sarris reaffirmed his commitment to auteur theory in *The American Cinema* only the year before, even there one senses a certain regret over having become auteurism's official spokesperson, and a concerted withdrawal from that role. It is understandable that, for the rest of his career, Sarris reacted to queries about his role in propagating auteur theory with a wary defensiveness. He was quite right to note the disproportion of the attacks and to object that he had never been a party-line auteurist in the first place. Indeed, one could say, for the paucity of its defenders in the United States, that auteur theory was a party line without a party.

What unleashed this onslaught? "Notes on Auteur Theory in 1962" is a gingerly outline that codifies three main tenets. Though Sarris credits the theory with reshaping his thinking about cinema, he makes no proprietary claims. On the contrary, he presents the theory as already established, preceding his tentative gloss, though—ritualizing the gesture that would precede excurses on auteurism ever after—he complains that there is no definition in English and that the theory itself is vexingly vague. For all that, he does nothing to suggest that he is about to supply the missing definition or clarify the vagueness. Rather, he credits the *Cahiers* critics for propounding auteurism and proceeds to extrapolate from their work a few modest principles. Distinguishing auteur theory from a "straightforward" theory of directors, Sarris asserts its contextual foundations, its penchant to consider individual films in relation to directors' evolving bodies of work, and claims it is "a pattern theory in constant flux" that would require great effort to validate, with little sense that he has any intention of taking on that labor. That Sarris's cautious account of a developing set of ideas was so widely read as proclaiming a holy writ inscribed in ignoble stone attests mostly to how embattled notions of cinematic value remained at the time he wrote.

Just as Sarris's early work as a whole shows the spotty influence of the *Cahiers* critics, "Notes on Auteur Theory" suggests a thorough yet selective reading of auteurists' work, reflecting the year Sarris spent in France just before writing the essay. "The first premise of auteur theory," Sarris writes, "is the technical competence of the director as a criterion of value."[33] This claim seems to translate the notion of efficacy that recurs often in auteurist writing of the 1950s. Jim Hillier cites this baseline appeal to the "efficacious" as one of the "qualities [the auteurists] find lacking in French cinema" (21). Rohmer, for example, writes, "If I had to characterize the American style of cinema, I would forward the two words *efficacy* and *elegance*" (89, emphasis in original). This admiration for basic proficiency is common among the *Cahiers* critics, however unlikely it may seem as a springboard into spheres of inspiration. The other two premises that Sarris codifies depend on the notion of abstraction—a concept which, as we have seen, figures centrally in auteurist notions of film style and form. In Sarris's model, it underlies both "the distinguishable personality of the director as a criterion of value" and the "interior meaning ... extrapolated from the tension between a director's personality and his material."[34] Sarris aptly observes and intermittently follows the auteurist propensity to extrapolate (a tendency that would especially outrage his critics) and to delight in discovering occulted meanings, especially as they emerge in relations among a given filmmaker's works. His view of the productive role of constraint, however, is more straightforward than that of the *Cahiers* critics, linked almost entirely to industry demands. On this basis, Sarris finds that a Hollywood craftsman like George Cukor has articulated a more abstract style than an art-cinema maven like Ingmar Bergman, who develops his own scripts. Though Sarris seems sporadically attuned to the dynamic kinaesthetics of auteurism, he locates abstraction mainly in the gaps between a script and its realization. His remarks echo in passing the *Cahiers* writers' fascination with the ineffable, as when he notes that "interior meaning" is ambiguous (that Bazinian term) because it is so integral to cinema and difficult to render in non-cinematic terms. Yet his "abstraction" remains a simplified version of theirs. Indeed, later in his career, Sarris takes a hard line on such matters: "Abstract aesthetics, especially on cinema, is generally the unreadable in search of the indescribable."[35]

Sarris was certainly engaged in translating auteurism into a new idiom, but his main concern ultimately was to adapt it, to convert it into a tool for his own critical practice and a system of wholesale classification. This was an important step in generalizing the word "auteur" to refer to virtually any film director, rather than maintaining it as a term of exclusion, a special honorific for a select few. As he makes clear in the introduction to *The American Cinema*, Sarris's essential intention is to co-opt auteurism to construct a model of film history oriented around directors, with "auteur theory" standing as a prompt to endless further research, a provocation to completism. American film history would quickly move beyond Sarris's value-saturated variant, a virtual prototype of the "great man" model. Even so, Sarris was astute in perceiving auteurism as a theory of value at its core, or—more specifically—a theory of revaluation, a call to reconsider the most basic assumptions about what makes a great film "great."

Echoes of the *Cahiers* writers persist through this early phase of Sarris's career in his recurrent idea that we remember moments and fragments more than whole films, and that cinema at its best resembles a species of poetry. The auteurists were working toward a theory of the fragment in film as surely as theorists like Siegfried Kracauer and Walter Benjamin had been earlier in culture at large; their sense of films' capacity to encompass poetry had everything to do with their sense of the transient experience of films, the poignant evanescence of their images, the intense yet fractional, ungraspable ways they haunt memory. Sarris is certainly correct to observe that neither Truffaut nor any of his comrades in arms mounts any systematic history of the American cinema. Indeed, the *Cahiers* writers devoted themselves mainly to the deeply contingent encounters between the systems of cinema's machineries and industries, and the errant, vagrant moments, the astonishments they made possible, however implausibly. What Sarris confers on auteurism is a conventional valorization of aesthetic coherence, a priority at odds with the main lines of *Cahiers* writing. Despite his brisk nod to the lure of the fragment that drew his French predecessors, Sarris ultimately vows that the critic must aspire to totality and so, as *The American Cinema* makes clear, must the auteur.

Sarris's rankings align roughly with the estimations of the *Cahiers* writers, judging by their writings and the best-films-of-the-year lists they began publishing in 1951, though some of his judgments reflect a distinct lag in this influence. Several of their most lauded auteurs—Aldrich, Mann, Preminger, and Ray—are denied entry into Sarris's pantheon and consigned to the second rung as "underrated stylists." From his vantage point a decade beyond the undaunted assessments of the *Cahiers* writers, Sarris seems less convinced of their extravagant endorsements. Sarris finds that Preminger failed to sufficiently transcend his material in his work of the 1960s, for example, or that Mann's style outstripped his meaning, or that Ray had become such a *cause célèbre* for auteur theory that it was impossible to maintain a sense of proportion about his career. All in all, Sarris finds himself in the unenviable position of having caught the infectious enthusiasm of 1950s auteurism but nursing ineluctable second thoughts that oblige him to reassert stuffy principles of moderation, a gallant stand for common sense that did nothing to prevent his critics from casting him, not his forebears, as the trendy wastrel.

Compared to the *Cahiers* auteurists, Sarris brings a more pragmatic (not to say literal-minded) eye to his accounts of directors' careers and an incomparably more conventional aesthetic to the judgments of films. Writing on Robert Mulligan in *The American Cinema*, he contradicts Truffaut's high opinion, finding that Mulligan's films lack coherence and boil down to stray bits and pieces of lyricism—just the bits and pieces that Truffaut would have cherished, of course, without worrying about the wholes. On McCarey, too, Sarris observes that "his moments may outlive his movies" but allows that "after enough great moments ... a personal style must be assumed even though it is difficult to describe."[36] The air of something sheepishly obligatory about this concession typifies Sarris's bemused response to many of the most characteristic enthusiasms of 1950s auteurism and the brash conviction of their expression. For Sarris, those valuations often translated as a form of esoterica—as reflected in the blunt yet perplexed qualification to his dismissal of that most definitive of auteurist test cases: "Alfred Hitchcock's *Marnie* is a failure by any standard but the most esoteric."[37]

While the *Cahiers* writers embraced (and later created) a cinema of "bits and pieces" to subvert hidebound standards, Sarris cultivated a traditional aesthetic that placed him ultimately much closer to the critical establishment than to the auteurist insurrection against it. While the auteurists joyously threw aside fogeyish crutches like the old dramatic unities, Sarris persevered in his dutiful search for coherence, dispensing chipper, witty brickbats for all that failed to achieve it. The auteurists rethought notions of success and coherence, while Sarris set about carefully parsing his judgments into "good" and "bad" reviews. The *Cahiers* writers tried to overhaul the whole value system of cinema; Sarris proceeded as if a few modest adjustments to a basically standard blueprint of taste was sufficient to do justice to that effort.

Just as "Notes on Auteur Theory" appeared in print, *Film Quarterly* ran a symposium on the question of "Personal Creation in Hollywood: Can It Be Done?" A panel consisting of critics as well as directors and producers (John Houseman, Irvin Kershner, Kent MacKenzie, Fred Zinnemann) treated the question as if they had never heard of such a thing as an auteur. The European art film versus American mass culture axis that the *Cahiers* writers tried to deconstruct remains firmly in place here, with the guiding assumption that European filmmakers have greater freedom to make "personal" films than Hollywood directors, the general notion of a personal film being one that makes recognizable "statements" and "comments" about social issues.

Houseman notes, for example, that "there is a very strong resistance to individual statements in American pictures, while on the other hand among the worst European picture-makers ... there is almost always some kind of personal statement."[38] A little known critic named Pauline Kael participates gamely in the proceedings, seeming to buy into the basic premises. A year later she would help to make "auteur" a buzzword by publishing in the same journal an all-out attack on Sarris and "auteur theory." The editors introduced her piece "Circles and Squares" with a perplexed and muddled account of French auteurism and a disapproving take on its influence: "In its homeland the *politique* has led to many peculiar judgments: it is Samuel Fuller, Nicholas Ray, and Otto Preminger who figure as the gods in this new pantheon. The results upon export are turning out to be even more peculiar."[39] The piece that followed would become the most notorious parry in the anti-auteurist counterblast.

Most surprising about Kael's scrappy polemic is how much she concedes at the outset. Not only does she grant as an article of faith filmmakers' status as "artist"—a word she uses more freely than Sarris does—but she confers authorial rank on directors, even disfavored ones, without batting an eye. She refers, as an apparent reflex, to "the John Ford films," "movies by George Cukor or Howard Hawks," "Irving Rapper films," "Mervyn LeRoy films." LeRoy was at best a fringe figure in the auteurist canon-in-the-making, while nobody ever dubbed Rapper an auteur, yet Kael's breezy inventory plunks them all down on a seemingly level playing field as putative progenitors, if not full-fledged creators and owners of their respective productions. Only in passing does Kael note the problem of collaboration that was grist for so many other critical mills. Whatever qualms she lodged against the auteur theory, her own blithe elevation of the director to the principal creative position could only mitigate them. Nor is she especially exercised about the auteurist penchant for tracing motifs from film to film, noting that this is common for critics in any art form.

What outrages Kael is not the method but the matter, the underlying assumptions—the very stuff of the "auteur theory" as *theory*. Among its early critics, Kael was virtually alone in acknowledging the conceptual bases of auteurism. She highlights its recondite tendencies and chides its elusive mixture of idealism and skepticism. Above all, she gleans the auteurist challenge to the most fundamental terms of conventional aesthetic judgment, at least where the cinema was concerned. For her, the offenses of auteur theory were affronts against taste. What is most "reprehensible," according to Kael, is the auteurists' inability to exercise taste and judgment even in their own preferences regarding the B-movies and Westerns they celebrated. The kinds of films the auteurists valued were bad enough—the cheap, lurid B-movies and studio-stamped genre films—but for Kael the worst of it was that they could not tell the wheat from the chaff even in that arid field. To these lapses, Kael counters her own blunt, unequivocal judgments on a polarized spectrum divided between the "good" and the "bad": *High Sierra* (1941) is "not a very good movie"; "It is an insult to an artist to praise his bad work along with his good"; with a "bad" script, "at best, [a director] can make an entertaining bad movie"; "It is as absurd to praise Lang's recent bad work as to dismiss Huston's early good work." Despite the curt tone, Kael pinpoints in that last dig a key issue in these debates, suggesting a greater awareness of the larger stakes than her treatment otherwise indicates. Both Lang and Huston *were*, of course, crucial test cases for the auteurist revaluation of American cinema. The critical establishment in the United States, such as it was, deemed Huston a director of quality, a position consolidated in James Agee's 1950 profile of Huston, "Undirectable Director"—a year before Agee collaborated with Huston as screenwriter on *The African Queen* (1951). As the title suggests, Agee's article was a virtual hagiography, portraying Huston as an uncompromising maverick who triumphed over the crippling constraints of a corrupt industry. One of the earliest journalistic celebrations of the putative independence of a filmmaker working within the studio system, the piece stands as a prototype for the legion of post-auteurist brandings of powerful directors in the New Hollywood, with Huston as a precedent for the Young Turks of that era.

For the auteurists, of course, "quality" was a loaded term, especially as deployed by critical establishments, and the auteurist denigration of Huston had everything to do with his reputation for quality in relation to his literary sensibility.

Most of Huston's films were adaptations, and his style shifted from project to project based on the variable demands of particular sources, from the hard-boiled momentum of *The Maltese Falcon* (1941), to the stoical hysterics of *In This Our Life* (1942), the ashen fatalism of *Treasure of the Sierra Madre* (1948), the achy "sensitivity" of *Red Badge of Courage* (1953), or the epic, swaggering overreach of *Moby-Dick* (1955). Huston's much-maligned adaptation of Herman Melville's novel served as an occasion for *Cahiers* to demolish Huston once and for all. As it happened, *Moby-Dick* found few supporters anywhere, though American critics on the whole viewed it as a false step in a generally admirable career, while for Rohmer and his peers, it only confirmed an overall paucity of cinematic invention, an inveterate literalness of mind, a proclivity to trump up "quality" by association with literary prestige. By 1957, in a *Cahiers* editorial roundtable, Huston was flatly declared finished.

The same year, Lang's high position in the *Cahiers* pantheon was certified in Rivette's review of Lang's *Beyond a Reasonable Doubt*. We have seen how that essay typifies auteurist esteem, but it also exemplifies the extreme divergence between *Cahiers* scales of value and those of American critics of the day, who disparaged Lang's film as a B-movie with a ludicrously contrived plot. Even when Lang's direction was exempted from the overall censure, it was damned with faint praise, the pained lenience due to the sense of a formerly great filmmaker in decline. Rivette's tribute, meanwhile, reaches its hushed apotheosis with this severe gambit: "Anyone who fails to be more moved by this film than by such appeals for sympathy [as Federico Fellini's] knows nothing, not only of cinema but of man" (142).

The drastic disparities here define auteurist debates of the time, and Rivette strikingly prefigures in his panegyric one of Kael's saltiest parries. In her rejoinder to Sarris, Kael avers that the works auteur critics call masterpieces often seem to reveal, for Kael, the director's contempt for the audience. But what American critics like her saw as cheap and lusterless in a movie like *Beyond a Reasonable Doubt* Rivette perceived as "pure," austere, the "abstract" poetry of a work that guides us into a "pitiless world" where "the only possible attitude of the creator must be one of *absolute contempt*" (142, emphasis in original). Both register the "contempt"—doubly uncanny, considering Lang's appearance as a misanthropic version of himself in Godard's 1963 film of that name—but what Kael understands as pathetic artistic impoverishment Rivette sees as consummate, a shattering series of conceptual "denials"— of reason, of verisimilitude, of ordinary pictorial beauty— growing inevitably out of the only philosophical position viable in Lang's uncompromised, intransigent worldview: "All these denials ... are conducted with a sort of disdain which some have been tempted to see as the filmmaker's contempt for the undertaking; why not, rather, for this kind of spectator?"— the kind, that is, who prefers a simple evening's entertainment (or Fellini) to an obdurate experiment in truth-telling that discloses "a transcendental order of experience" (140–141).

Though Kael could hardly have been well versed in French auteurism, she granted immunity from her critique to the *Cahiers* critics, on the grounds that their theory responded to the energies and crude power of Hollywood movies. For Kael, the French strain was vaguely explicable as the reflection of an exoticized image of America from an estranged cultural perspective prone to error—a faintly condescending attitude of the why-do-the-French-love-Jerry-Lewis variety, to which Rivette's stern accolade, among countless examples, gives the lie. As Kael also argues, European directors work in circumstances more comparable to theater directors in the United States, a privilege that obstructs an understanding of the intricate power relations in the American film industry.

It is the concept of "interior meaning" that prompts Kael's most furious consternation. Though Sarris highlights the concept, he provides little theoretical grounding for it, giving Kael polemical opportunities that she seizes with robust glee. She chides the alleged redundancy of the idea: Where else would meaning reside if not internally, she asks—a curious query from one who became unusually preoccupied with oppositions between surface and depth in her own subsequent work. Finally, the notion of interior meaning comes to represent the whole "mystique" Kael imputes to auteur theory, a word she uses derisively to denote both an unsavory mysticism and an unseemly collusion with fashion and celebrity culture. For Kael, a given filmmaker's auteur status—his "élan of the soul," in a phrase of Sarris's that Kael mocks with special vehemence—relies on some undefinable quality that recalls the "It" of high fashion. Kael's point is that auteur theory co-opts that discourse and gussies it up in a pseudo-intellectual garb.

To illustrate the concept of interior meaning, Sarris points to two scenes in different films by the same director, Raoul Walsh. He identifies striking similarities between a breezy comedy, *Every Night at Eight* (1935), and a grim proto-noir, *High Sierra*; in both, the hero talks in his sleep, overheard by a female character from whom he has been hiding feelings he reveals in his nocturnal mutterings. From this parallel Sarris infers a relation that becomes a gauge of Walsh's "personality." Kael notes snidely—and rightly—that Sarris could easily have perceived the connection without the aid of an abstruse theory, but what she does not grasp is how proudly and defiantly the auteurists brandished this very abstruseness. Despite Sarris's exaltation of interior meaning as "the ultimate glory of the cinema," his squeamish treatment suggests a level of discomfort with the concept equal to his fascination with it. Sarris celebrates the recondite aspects of auteur theory in his essay, and his explication of interior meaning emphasizes its ineffable character, evading paraphrase. He defines it mostly by what it is not—or "not exactly": "a vision of the world" or direct expression of directorial attitudes. From Sarris's examples, recalling the *Cahiers* writers more closely than usual, it seems that interior meaning emerges in moments of epiphany, when individual films suddenly disclose some elusive, intensified conduit to something beyond themselves, an element that taps into the very "stuff of cinema."

In retrospect, it was clear that Kael was uniquely unsuited to do justice to auteur theory. Her subsequent career as a film

critic was virtually defined by her own energetic advocacy of
directors devalued by other critics, from Brian De Palma to Sam
Peckinpah and Irvin Kershner. It was not the "auteur" angle
that irked her; it was the *theory* that made her, like Hitchcock's
Marnie, see red. The year before "Circles and Squares," Kael
had published another broadside, "Is There a Cure for Film
Criticism?" As it happened, the piece was not really about
criticism but, in the guise of an inhospitable review of Siegfried
Kracauer's *Theory of Film* (1960), a frontal assault on film
theory. Though Kael accuses Kracauer of unusual priggishness,
her approach denigrates theory itself as an intellectual activity,
and film theory especially as poisonously pedantic, a violation
of cinema's basic pleasure principle. To be sure, Kracauer may
have been guilty of the same idealistic "Platonism" of which the
auteurists stood accused; his book's subtitle, "The Redemption
of Physical Reality," aptly suggests the contours of his model, a
post-Bazinian and implicitly modernist redefinition of cinematic
realism, positing the cinema as a kind of vast, virtual archive
preserving fragments of reality that would otherwise have
been lost. Such sweeping conceptions could only prove vexing
to the pragmatic particularist, especially since the provenance
of Kracauer's thought corresponded at points with those of
auteurism. Sections of Kracauer's work in progress appeared
in *Film Culture,* the same periodical that first published
Sarris's "Notes on Auteur Theory," a journal dedicated to the
promotion of vanguard sensibilities in the discourse around
cinema. For her part, Kael harbored a basic hostility for most
manifestations of cinematic modernism, whether it was the
outright avant-gardism of Ron Rice or Stan Brakhage (both
of whom she disparages in "Circles and Squares") or the art
cinema of Ingmar Bergman or Alain Resnais. In the end, her
own unyielding view of cinema as a fundamentally popular art
demanded that she refute "auteur theory."

As a sidebar to Kael's piece, *Film Quarterly* printed a brief
excerpt from a review of Vincente Minnelli's *Two Weeks in
Another Town* (1962) from a publication identified as the
main vehicle (along with *Film Culture*) of American auteurism.

The *New York Film Bulletin* appeared from 1960 to 1964, starting as a mimeographed zine of a thousand copies and expanding into a printed monthly (though its publication was always spotty) with a circulation of 12,000, "the largest of any American film magazine," according to the editors (n. 44, inside front cover).[40] The publication boldly trumpeted its own position "as the U.S. outlet for the new critical viewpoint that started in France and so quickly and controversially has taken root in England" with its "radical reviews and features, translated reprints from *Cahiers du Cinéma*, and sometimes acid comments on the film scene ... " (n. 41, inside front cover). Covering screenings of local film societies, revival houses, museums, and even television stations, as well as reviewing new films, with frequently unsigned contributions, the magazine promoted a version of movie love as cultish connoisseurship, with contributors routinely commenting on films as objects, remarking on the quality of prints, the circumstances of television broadcasts, and other material factors. The tone is impudent and campy, treating the Hollywood mainstream with comic vitriol but also directing irreverent gibes even at sacred cows of auteurism. Some items parody gossip columns: "It has been reported from a non-reliable source that the scenes involving the battle sequences from *Ben-Hur* [1959] had to be re-shot four times. The Yugoslavian Cavalry, especially hired for this assignment ... were severely chastised for ruining the first three takes. It seems that they kept upstaging Charlton Heston" (n. 12–14, 3). This parry has the advantage of not only slighting the redoubtable William Wyler (who directed *Ben-Hur* and was an auteurist bugbear) but slamming the *Cahiers* lionization of Heston as an axiom whose presence in any film instilled beauty.

Many key auteurist attitudes are retained, however, including a version of its canon-in-progress, a casually audacious and jokey adoption of extreme positions, a fetishism of technique, a disdain for "social conscience" filmmaking and, by extension, for British film and film culture: John Schlesinger's *A Kind of Loving* (1962), for example, is fiercely dismissed as being "in the tradition of truly horrible British fucked-up cinema" (v. 2,

n. 2, 22). With its withering take on the film as a whole and paradoxical glorification of its director, this review of Nicholas Ray's *King of Kings* (1961) could have sprung right from the pages of *Cahiers*: It "is a long B picture with a C cast and an atrocious score Miklos Rosza had left over from the dregs of *Ben-Hur*. It is pointless to itemize the deficiencies of such a hopeless project, but Ray's visual technique never falters … He remains one of the most exciting directors in the world" (v. 3, n. 1, 5). Or this read on Welles's *Mr. Arkadin*: "Granted that one must be 'committed' to Welles to even like *Arkadin*, but once one has made the commitment, there is no choice but to call it a masterpiece" (n. 45, 21). The latter observation suggests a more distanced perspective on the terms and turns of "the New Criticism," as they called it; there is frequently in the *Bulletin* a tacit acknowledgment of something slightly absurd about auteurism and about the cultural politics of taste. Indeed, the contributors are much more willing than the *Cahiers* writers to concede that movies they love, including auteurs' products, might very well resemble "trash" (a word Kael too would convert into a kind of praise in years to come). *Two Weeks in Another Town*, for instance, marries a piece of "respectable trash" like the Irwin Shaw novel it is based on with the talents of "a director who respects trash": Minnelli has "taken something not fit for even the slightest bit of serious critical attention and turned it into a film that demands exhaustive visual analysis" (n. 45, 23). As a result, "Minnelli is fast challenging Douglas Sirk's title as Hollywood's 'King of Camp'" (23). This open celebration of Camp (two years before Susan Sontag's famous "Notes on 'Camp'") no doubt reflects the work of gay contributors like Carlos Clarens, who would go on memorably to queer horror in his auteurist-inflected *Illustrated History of the Horror Film* (1967), and it marks a significant turn in auteurist taste. For the writers at the *New York Film Bulletin*, movies were a kind of pop memorabilia recast as art through the pleasures of camp/cult spectatorship, providing a bridge between the renegade modernism of the *Cahiers* writers and the pop-cult absolutism of Pauline Kael.

Leo McCarey redivivus, or the making of an unlikely auteur

In one of its most significant early issues, the *New York Film Bulletin* published substantial work by a cadre of British writers who would go on to found *Movie*. Ian Cameron, V. F. Perkins, and Mark Shivas interviewed Joseph Losey at length, while Robin Wood, in one of his first publications, contributed a piece on auteurism suggestively called "The New Criticism," which he understood essentially as oriented around mise-en-scène: "[A]n analysis of mise-en-scène is the only valid way of assessing a film's significance in relation to life, the moral and spiritual values it embodies" (series 2, n. 12–14, 25). As this remark suggests, Wood's critical approach, and those of the *Movie* staff generally, would be incomparably more earnest than that of the *Cahiers* writers, shot through with a righteous streak, an impatience with frivolities of the sort the *Cahiers* writers routinely indulged. For Wood, questions of evaluation are intrinsically moral, the devaluation of a Hitchcock, therefore, a wrong that needed to be set right. At the same time, despite a donnish severity creeping in intermittently, he routinely traversed levels of culture as if they simply did not exist (which, of course, they didn't, except as discourse). For the rest of his career, Wood continued his campaign to rescue unjustly maligned films and reputations, from exploitation-derived horror films of the 1960s and 1970s (George Romero, Brian De Palma, and so on) to disreputable grindhouse-meisters like Larry Cohen or Stephanie Rothman.

The main contributions of this group to the development of auteurism, however, were less about the dynamics of evaluation and revaluation than about putting the "theory" into practice. In 1965, Wood published his landmark *Hitchcock's Films*, initiating a wave of auteurist-influenced director studies over the following fifteen years. Wood certainly contributed to a rehabilitation of Hitchcock's reputation from "popular entertainer" to "serious artist." He did so, however, by showing the films to repay extensive analysis, demonstrating that sustained attention to mise-en-scène in, say, *Marnie* could expose previous verdicts against that film as hasty and superficial, if not insensitive and philistine. The writers of the *New York Film Bulletin* may have believed that *Two Weeks in Another Town* "demands exhaustive visual analysis," but they no more provided it than the *Cahiers* writers ever had (with obvious exceptions like Chabrol and Rohmer's own book on Hitchcock). That would be left to the British wing, which provided among the first and best models of long-form auteurist criticism, or film criticism of any kind (and, not incidentally, one of the most suggestive models for the analysis that follows in the next chapter). *Movie* was a kind of hybrid academic/mainstream periodical that featured extended essays on individual films aspiring to exhaustive interpretation as well as to some engagement with the feelings and textures of given films. Once the magazine had published a few numbers, this enterprise seemed much less counterintuitive than it had only a short time before. The idea that a movie might be worth discussing at length in print, even if that worth was still dependably certified by the presence of an auteur, quickly came to seem commonplace, laying groundwork for film studies as a discipline with its own kind of "research."

Due in part to these expansions of auteurism across many lines, Leo McCarey's pedigree was more complicated than most. Though he was in the first generation of Hollywood filmmakers, he resided in the second generation of Hollywood auteurs. This deferral makes him an exemplary figure for our purposes because it highlights the variable terms by which such reputations are constructed and the contingencies around which any canon gets made. Throughout the 1950s and 1960s, McCarey's status as an auteur was less secure than most because his work lacked both the ironic edge of the more self-reflexive cadre (Hitchcock, Ophuls, Nicholas Ray, Sirk, Sternberg, Welles) or the grandeur and sweep of the mythmakers (Ford, Mann, Vidor, Walsh). The straightforward manner of McCarey's work goes a long way toward explaining why his annexation into the auteurist canon was late in coming. It would have been a fool's errand to try to reinvent him as a quasi-modernist, and the melancholy overtones of his films were too withdrawn to qualify him for immediate entry. His support of square principles like patriotism, individualism, and old-school democratic ideals hardly served to enhance his auteurist appeal in theory.

As an initial canon of auteurs took shape, McCarey mostly hovered at the periphery. He was mentioned only in passing in *Cahiers* issues of the 1950s, though his name cropped up on ten-best lists, with Chabrol citing *Affair to Remember* in 1958 and *Rally Round the Flag Boys!* appearing in the magazine's official tally in 1959. (Ultimately, *An Affair to Remember* would be the lone McCarey film to appear in the *Cahiers* list of the hundred greatest films of all time.) *Cahiers* did not accord McCarey full auteur treatment until 1965, when it published a long interview with McCarey by Serge Daney and Jean-Louis Noames followed by a critical piece signed by Noames (though reflecting a clear Daneyan influence) and a complete filmography. Daney and Noames were foremost among the 1960s generation of *Cahiers* writers dedicated to keeping the tradition of 1950s auteurism alive after most of its former stalwarts had migrated to filmmaking. Noames's piece is a genuine throwback, recalling the paradoxical manner and stylistic delirium of a Rivette on Hawks, say, or a Godard on Nicholas Ray. Admirers of McCarey might be forgiven for failing to recognize him in this animated treatment, but any student of auteurism could certainly place the approach, with its adrenalized exhumation of the works' darkest undertones.

Noames portrays McCarey as an anarchic primitive who builds a "universe" populated by "strange beings, beasts," propelled by an aesthetic of the hollow or empty (*creux*) that "takes life as an obstacle and the cinema as a pretext for overcoming it," and at the same time casts him as a cinematic dreamer, a purveyor alongside Raoul Walsh of "the same reverie on the cinema, corrected … with the difference that in McCarey, pleasure is revealed in the dream, until it fades to evanescence, while in Walsh, offenses are re-lived by dint of the same modification and erasure."[41] More securely anointed figures are enlisted to usher McCarey into the company of auteurs. Quoted to the effect that "you'd have to be crazy to want to make cinema," Fritz Lang is cited as a comrade in lunacy to McCarey's purported dedication to "supporting in his films that which he cannot tolerate (and which we cannot tolerate), that is, life in its unbearable impossibility." In light of this commitment, ultimately, McCarey is "naturally enough … led to tolerate what he has supported … reaching through dementia." Meanwhile, the "arbitrary mating" of the "obliquely deformed beings" who make up the casts, especially considering the "incompatibility of the participants," is said to be a "Cukorian ambition," except that in McCarey "physical love is impossible." Even if the characters are "monsters more than men," says Noames, "this does not prevent the latter from carrying the hope and characteristic intelligence" of McCarey's work. Like many auteurist narratives, this account of McCarey's career clearly reads backward from the bleaker standpoint of the director's late work; even though *My Son John* is not mentioned in the piece, it seems central to those of Noames's premises that look more dubious when applied to earlier work.

Despite the belatedness of this acknowledgment, Pauline Kael—as if naming names before HUAC—had already sarcastically cited McCarey two years earlier as one of the unaccountable auteurist darlings in "Circles and Squares." Still innocent of Kael's brewing operation plan, meanwhile, Sarris published a long dossier in the same season's special issue on American cinema of *Film Culture*, airing a practice exercise for the directorial rankings of *The American Cinema*. In 1963, Sarris placed McCarey in the third line; by the time *The American Cinema* was published five years later, he had elevated the director to the second rung. Twenty years later, Sarris remarked that he might still have underrated McCarey, though the only higher rank would have been the first.[42] Meanwhile, when *Movie* began publishing in 1962, it included from its first issues directorial rankings from "Great," to "Brilliant," "Very Talented," "Talented," and "Competent or Ambitious." Following the *Cahiers* line, the "Great" category contained only two figures, Hawks and Hitchcock. The "Brilliant" (second) class then featured several directors including McCarey; ten years later, in the revised canon in an anthology of work from the magazine, the "Brilliant" class had been severely winnowed, containing only two filmmakers— McCarey and Orson Welles.[43] Even so, the director went unmentioned in the rest of the volume, and *Movie* devoted not a single article to McCarey's work for the entirety of its run.

McCarey's most consistent auteurist supporter during this time, however, was an important *Movie* contributor. Robin Wood published two significant essays on McCarey in the 1970s, and an extended critical overview of his work in his *Sexual Politics and Narrative Film* that absorbs and amplifies that earlier material, a major treatment with an air of culmination, of being the last word on its subject. The earlier pieces celebrate McCarey's spontaneity and improvisatory spirit and his democratizing impulses, comparing his work to Jean Renoir's while finding that the latter is a more self-conscious artist. Wood goes even further in his later piece, placing McCarey among the major artists of the cinema. His approach there recalls Noames's *Cahiers* piece, viewing McCarey's apparent allegiances to patriotic ideals and "family values" as profoundly ambivalent and reading the films against the grain of such attitudes, as ideologically subversive texts— mostly excepting the "unforgivable" *My Son John*. Even Wood, however, denies McCarey the self-consciousness that was the ultimate hallmark of the true auteur. McCarey himself, muses Wood, "might have been hauled before a committee on 'un-American activities' if his films had been properly understood; if he had permitted himself to fully understand them, he might have felt compelled to make a full confession, then retreat into alcoholism long before he actually did."[44]

One of the most useful after-effects of auteurism was to challenge the idea that American movies could always be counted on to serve the dominant social order in some direct or singleminded way. The *Cahiers* editors' collective text on *Young Mr. Lincoln* (1939) in 1969 may have been intended as the last nail in the coffin, the magazine's official repudiation of the *politique des auteurs*, but the acknowledgment of John Ford's role as an important agent in the articulation of the film's value systems contributes to what became in effect the new editorial policy, a commitment to ideological critique based on an understanding of ideology as fundamentally multivalent.[45] The same year, in the influential *Cahiers* essay "Cinema/ Ideology/Criticism," Jean-Louis Comolli and Jean Narboni laid down the magazine's influential schema defining a spectrum from "a" to "g," from total saturation with the ideology of the dominant order to complete resistance to it, with the former type of film to be rejected and the latter to be supported.[46] In the short run the class that drew the most interest was also the one that encompassed the greatest number of examples, the so-called "category e." This designation comprised films superficially complicit with prevailing ideology that also evinced significant subtextual resistance to it, an undeniably post-auteurist ranking in the sense that so many items in the tally had been favorites of the 1950s *Cahiers* writers.

Is McCarey a worthy denizen of "category e"? Contributors to *Movie* were on the whole more taken with the designation through the 1970s and 1980s (with Andrew Britton leading the charge) than contributors to *Cahiers* in the same period, and Wood's reading of McCarey is very much in that spirit. The few other post-auteurist critical treatments of McCarey's work also lean in this direction, ranging from celebrations of the director's anarchic proclivities to readings of *The Bells of St. Mary's* as a commentary on the church's repressiveness shot through with a sexual current between Father O'Malley and Sister Superior. Rich and persuasive as such readings may be, McCarey's primary claims to a place in auteurist pantheons, given his work's lack of commonality with the other main exhibits, had more to do with what his work did *not* do than what it did. Had there ever been an ideal auteurist text, it would have been stylistically flamboyant and formally self-reflexive, imbued with eroticism and a fetishistic ambience if also rigorously resistant to them, fascinated by the operations of power and unforgiving of its effects, emotionally abundant, stylized, visceral yet detached.

McCarey falls short on almost every count. The world he evokes is virtually sexless, which is why nuns and priests take their places in it so naturally. To say that his characters lack ambition is an understatement. The palpable delight that many of his couples take in each other resides in this very absence of aspiration; as Wood notes, they really just want to play together, and when they are allowed to, the movies they're in all but purr with pleasure, as in the Manhattan interlude of *Make Way for Tomorrow* or the shipboard scenes of *Love Affair*. This is true even when it seems otherwise; in *Good Sam,* the wife who frets about her husband's irresponsibility must learn to put aside those qualms and see him with new eyes as he "really is." This entreaty—to cast off such worries and see the other afresh—is just about the only obligation the films are willing to impose upon their characters. Wood claims that McCarey dislikes families but loves couples, and it is certainly true that the characters treated most critically in his work—more critically, in a way, than the Nazi played by Walter Slezak in *Once Upon a Honeymoon*—are the children of the couple in *Make Way for Tomorrow*. But Wood does not go far enough: McCarey is less interested in Hollywood romance and the traditional marriage plot than probably any other American director of his time. Three of his films do make courtship central to their narratives—*Indiscreet, Love Affair,* and its remake—but even in those cases, marriage looms as a threat, fraught with obligation, a terminus to be deferred. In the Laurel and Hardy films, *Six of a Kind, The Awful Truth, Good Sam, My Son John,* and *Rally Round the Flag Boys!*, marriage is depicted as an obstacle to the spontaneous emotional connection the films champion, a province of dreary responsibility and habituated drudgery.

This treatment does not really place McCarey too far outside the Hollywood norm, where the bickering couple and the battle-of-the-sexes are as much staples of comedy as the abusive relationship is of melodrama. It was in large part by attending to this unflattering depiction of marriage and family, apparently conventionalized into invisibility to native audiences, that the auteurists were able to excavate so much submerged material that seemed critical of American life *tout court*. Broadly speaking, one could say that comedies in the classical era end in marriage while melodramas show what happens next. The 1930s comedy-of-remarriage cycle was such a distinctive group of films because it found a way to make comic hay out of stories about already-married couples, but what made those movies so anomalous was that they had to separate the couples all over again to achieve that end. McCarey's films are essentially *about* divided couples, joined by temperament but sundered by circumstance, with marriage posited in many cases as the most salient factor in the split. The separation may be imposed (*Make Way for Tomorrow, The Bells of St. Mary's*), elected (*The Awful Truth, Love Affair, Affair to Remember*), or enforced by happenstance (*Once Upon a Honeymoon, Good Sam*), but in nearly every case the film insists that we see the members of the couple apart more than we see them together. Rarely have co-stars shared less screen time than in a post-Laurel-and-Hardy McCarey movie; the principals of *Love Affair* have only two scenes together in the film's second half, one lasting mere seconds, while Cary Grant and Ginger Rogers in *Once Upon a Honeymoon* appear in only a handful of scenes together, and Gary Cooper and Ann Sheridan too spend the bulk of *Good Sam* apart.

Make Way for Tomorrow and *Good Sam* are unlikely companion pieces considering the intense pathos of the earlier film and the erratic cheer of the latter. Between the two arcs a trajectory from the more conventionally focused and precise construction of McCarey's films of the 1930s and the increasingly more diffuse forms of his later work. Yet both concern couples of long standing whose relation reaches a crisis point. In *Make Way for Tomorrow*, Lucy (Beulah Bondi) and Bark (Victor Moore) are the elderly parents of five grown children when their house is repossessed at the height of the Great Depression, and they are forced to occupy separate quarters with their children's families, none of which will take both in. In *Good Sam*, the compulsive generosity of the title character (Gary Cooper) aggrieves his long-suffering wife Lu (Ann Sheridan) to the point of alienation. All are characters defined as set in their ways yet not obstinate or bull-headed even though they may be seen that way by others; in fact, it is those others who come in for unflattering treatment, like the children in *Make Way for Tomorrow* or Sam's obnoxious boss who cannot see how Sam's altruism boosts his bottom line. Not only does no member of either couple undergo significant changes in the course of the narrative, but the films go to some lengths to establish that no change is called for. In both cases the actors' performances convey an intimate mutual pleasure that each takes in the other—the way Bondi and Moore incline toward one another when they are together, for example, or Gary Cooper's offhanded little private grins when his wife berates him, or Sheridan's wry eye-rolling affection even at her most vexed.

What both films show is how these lovers *re*-learn this sense of pleasure, having lost touch with it through physical or emotional separation, each seeing anew the value of what the other "really is"—not what he or she *should be*, or might become. To this end *Make Way* takes an unanticipated (thus "McCareyian," in Serge Daney's coinage) and most welcome detour in its final third. Separated since the film's first scene, Lucy and Bark reunite, ditch the children, and embark on an impetuous odyssey together through New York City. They linger in the park, revisit the grand hotel where they honeymooned decades before, and go on a joyride in a fancy car. An aura of benevolence surrounds this enchanted interlude, the indignities Lucy and Bark have quietly endured at the hands of their children now mere wisps of a fog that has magically lifted. Everyone now welcomes them, everyone is kind—except for a lone wisecracker whose jokes at their expense mark him indelibly as an insufferable buffoon. The couple's inquisitive wanderings bespeak a restored freedom, with an imponderable sense of oppression surmounted, of time suspended. There is a breathless quality to these gossamer, delicate scenes, as if the slightest vapor could break the spell, and we know all the while that it will have to end—though the idyll is sustained beyond the point when any other director in the studio system (except perhaps Frank Borzage) would have dared to sustain it. In the back seat as their joyride comes to an end, Bark and Lucy improvise a rendition of "Let Me Call You Sweetheart," the same song Sam and Lu sing on their reunion at the end of *Good Sam* eleven years later. In both cases the duet is loveably awkward and off-key, befitting the song's function to signify a mutual accord, an ultimate acceptance of each by the other in spite of everything.

When couples become families, McCarey's interest flags and his affections attenuate. It is no exaggeration to suggest that the deepest impulse of the Hollywood mind-set is to marry off its heterosexuals, and even when McCarey's movies participate in this crusade, the sadness that underlies most of them and surfaces in many derives in large part from the ubiquity of this mandate and the consequences it decrees. The institutionalization of the couple alienates, driving out the spontaneity that united them. We could say that a McCarey film in which the characters succeed in reviving their original perceptions of each other is a comedy; the ones in which they fail to see each other anew are the tragedies. That formulation is too neat since there are really no tragedies and since comedy and drama blend so imperceptibly in these films, but in either case, a sense of equanimity attends the outcome. Even the ending of *The Bells of St. Mary's* partakes less than most Hollywood movies in a logic of redemption, the ordinary uplift of the "happy ending." McCarey almost never implies that his characters need to change—or that they could—only that they need to become and be seen as they "really are." What requires redemption, after all, is only what was not properly valued in the first place.

Notes

1   Roland Barthes, "The Death of the Author," in *Image/Music/Text*, trans. Stephen Heath (London: Fontana Press, 1977), 148.

2   Michel Foucault, "What Is an Author?" in *Aesthetics, Ethics, and Epistemology. Vol. II*, Robert Hurley et al., trans., James D. Faubion, ed. (New York: New Press, 1998), 207.

3   Ibid., 211.

4   See Richard Dyer, "Believing in Fairies: The Author and the Homosexual," in *Inside/Out: Lesbian Theories, Gay Theories*, Diana Fuss, ed. (New York: Routledge, 1991), 185–204; and Jane Gaines, "Of Cabbages and Authors," in *A Feminist Reader in Early Cinema*, Jennifer Bean and Diane Negra, eds. (Durham, NC: Duke University Press, 2002), 88–118.

5   George Kelly, *Craig's Wife* (Boston: Little, Brown, 1926), 17.

6   See Alexandre Astruc, "The Birth of a New Avant-Garde: La Camèra-Stylo," in *The French New Wave*, Peter Graham and Ginette Vincendeau, eds. (London: British Film Institute, 2009), 31–36; and Francois Truffaut, "A Certain Tendency of the French Cinema," in *Movies and Methods, vol. I*, Bill Nichols, ed. (Berkeley: University of California Press, 1974), 224–237.

7   Pascal Kamina, *Film Copyright in the European Union*, 2nd ed. (Cambridge: Cambridge University Press, 2016), 168. Much of the information in this paragraph derives from this source; see especially pages 36–42, 294–295.

8   Louis Chavance, "Birth and History of the International Federation of Film Auteurs," *Cahiers du Cinéma* no. 14 (July 1952): 17–24, translation mine; and Marcel L'Herbier, "Who Is the Auteur of the International Federation of Film Auteurs?" *Cahiers du Cinéma* no. 17 (November 1952): 25–34.

9   Pierre Bertin, "Thanks Returned to the Auteur," *Cahiers du Cinéma* no. 66 (February 1956): 40–41.

10 Jean Quéval, "The Auteurs Who Do Not Think of Themselves as Others," *Cahiers du Cinéma* no. 3 (June 1951): 46–47; and Jean Myrsine, "Gene Kelly as Film Auteur and One-Man-Band," *Cahiers du Cinéma* no. 14 (July 1952): 34–38.

11 Jacques Doniol-Valcroze, rev. of *Come Back, Little Sheba*,
    Cahiers du Cinéma no. 23 (May 1953): 49–51, my translation.

12 Michel Dorsday "The Cinema Is Dead," *Cahiers du Cinéma*
    no. 16 (October 1952): 55–58; and Chris Marker, "Letter from
    Hollywood," *Cahiers du Cinéma* no. 25 (July 1953): 26–34, my
    translations.

13 Eric Rohmer, "*Cahiers* Readers and the *Politique des Auteurs*,"
    Cahiers du Cinéma no. 63 (October 1956): 54–55, my
    translation.

14 Ibid., 54.

15 Ibid., 55.

16 André Bazin, *What Is Cinema? Vol. 1*, Hugh Gray, trans.
    (Berkeley: University of California Press, 2004), 71.

17 Ibid., xxi.

18 Jim Hillier ed., *Cahiers du Cinéma: The 1950s: Neo-Realism,
    Hollywood, New Wave* (Cambridge: Harvard University Press,
    1985), 99–100. This is the crucial source in English for *Cahiers*
    writing, and I have relied on it as a primary reference to avoid
    where possible citation of materials unavailable in translation.
    Page numbers of all further references are cited parenthetically
    in the text.

19 Jean-Luc Godard, *Godard on Godard*, Tom Milne, ed. and
    trans. (New York: Viking, 1972), 84.

20 Ibid., 115.

21 Ibid., 117.

22 Ibid., 61.

23 Eric Rohmer, *The Taste for Beauty*, Carol Volk, trans.
    (Cambridge: Cambridge University Press, 1990), 99.

24 Francois Truffaut, *The Films in My Life*, Leonard Mayhew,
    trans. (New York: Simon and Schuster, 1978), 120, emphasis in
    original.

25 Rohmer, "*Cahiers* Readers and the *Politique des Auteurs*," 54.

26 Rohmer, *Taste for Beauty*, 100.

27 John Hess, "La Politique des Auteurs," *Jump Cut* no. 2 (July/
    August 1974): 20–22.

28 Truffaut, *The Films of My Life*, 94.

29 Godard, *Godard on Godard*, 60–61.

30 Claude Chabrol and Eric Rohmer, *Hitchcock, the First Forty-Four Films*, Stanley Hochman, trans. (New York: Ungar, 1979), 43.

31 Rohmer, *Taste for Beauty*, 140, emphasis in original.

32 Ibid., 138–139.

33 Andrew Sarris, "Notes on the Auteur Theory in 1962," in *Film Culture Reader*, P. Adam Sitney, ed. (New York: Cooper Square Press, 2000), 132.

34 Ibid., 133.

35 Andrew Sarris, *The Primal Screen* (New York: Simon and Schuster, 1973), 66.

36 Andrew Sarris, *The American Cinema: Directors and Directions, 1929–1968* (New York: Da Capo Books, 1996), 100.

37 Andrew Sarris, *Confessions of a Cultist: On the Cinema, 1955–1969* (New York: Simon and Schuster, 1971), 141.

38 "Personal Creation in Hollywood: Can It Be Done?" Roundtable discussion. *Film Quarterly* 15, no. 3 (Spring 1962): 27–28.

39 Pauline Kael, "Circles and Squares," *Film Quarterly* 16, no. 3 (Spring 1963): 12.

40 Rare copies of *New York Film Bulletin* are located in the archival holdings of the Cinematic Arts Library at the University of Southern California, where I consulted them. Issue and page numbers are cited in the text.

41 Jean-Louis Noames, "The Art and Manner of Leo McCarey," *Cahiers du Cinéma* no. 163 (February 1965): 25–30, my translation. All quotations in the following paragraph are from this source.

42 Andrew Sarris, "Auteurism Turns Silver," *Village Voice* (7 June 1988): 99.

43 Ian Cameron, ed., *Movie Reader* (New York: Praeger, 1972), 9.

44 Robin Wood *Sexual Politics and Narrative Film: Hollywood and Beyond* (New York: Columbia University Press, 1998), 142.

45 "John Ford's *Young Mr. Lincoln*." Collective text by the editors of *Cahiers du Cinéma*. Helen Lackner and Diana Matias, trans. *Screen* 13, no. 3 (1972): 5–44.

46 Jean-Louis Comolli and Jean Narboni, "Cinema/Ideology/ Criticism," in *Screen Reader 1*, J. Ellis, ed. (London: Society for Education in Film and Television, 1977), 2–12.

CHAPTER TWO

The Strange Case of *My Son John*

A Leo McCarey film, or what becomes an auteur

Working most often in a minor key, McCarey embodied the modesty and lack of pretension that was a *Cahiers* baseline, but these were also, especially as auteurism gained traction and splintered in many directions, the traits generally shared among auteurs whose positions were most precarious, and the measures most prone to reconsideration, as witness the case of Jean-Luc Godard and Joseph L. Mankiewicz. A persistently earthbound quality grounds McCarey's work; though certainly a cinema of "moments," as Sarris and others remarked, it boasts few of the showy set pieces of a Hitchcock or Welles, little of the formal play of a Sirk or Tashlin—whose version of *Rally Round the Flag Boys!* (a project Tashlin was originally announced to direct) would surely have been a very different film from the plainspoken one that McCarey actually made. In McCarey's work, the moments are small, the narrative scales most often domestically inclined—a version of the directorial effacement McCarey cultivated in the Hal Roach studios as a semi-anonymous artisan lingered for much of his career.

One of the most basic ideas of 1950s auteurism was the assumption that a distinctive style could be culled from conventional elements of an industrial artistic mode with classical inclinations. The seeming transparency of McCarey's work might have made him, in this sense, a more quintessential auteur than those who stood most drastically against the norms of Hollywood, like von Stroheim or Welles. Like Capra or Cukor, McCarey was mainly content to be what he mostly was, a studio journeyman, a team player who wanted little more than to please the mass audience and satisfy the front office. Even the two films he made that proved to be the most problematic fits—*Make Way for Tomorrow* and *My Son John*—both tapped into the zeitgeist of their day, the former as a Depression-era tearjerker on the order of the immensely popular films of Frank Borzage, the latter an even more clearly made-to-order product of the McCarthy era. Even if neither project could properly be called calculated for mass approval— sincerity and conviction being a stock-in-trade of both—their respective "failures" could hardly have been predicted.

According to Sarris and others, McCarey represented a spirit of improvisation in American film. Though this aspect of his work has been exaggerated, since many of the allegedly improvised segments appear in the scripts, this principle is perhaps most visible at the level of performance but also pronounced through narrative and at the micro-levels of style where by common consent directorial signatures reside, in the textures and rhythms of shots, in the placement and movement of the camera, in the handling of scenes and sequences—in short, in the treatment of mise-en-scène. The rhythms most characteristic of McCarey's films alternate lags and lurches timed to defy expectation and resist conventional punctuation. For the most part, his films lack the snappy momentum of a Hawks or Capra, the punch-drunk, stop-and-start drive of a George Stevens or Busby Berkeley (with whom McCarey collaborated on *The Kid from Spain*), or the elegant languor of a Sternberg. A fleet, precise sense of movement is not unheard of in a McCarey scene, and effects of suddenness and surprise are quite common, like the quick pans he favors in place of reverse-shots. Often these effects are at unsettling odds—a tightly calibrated gag undermined by a quick, dissonant cut, an element of surprise deflected by a blithe, unforced shift in attention.

McCarey's editing style is loose, relaxed, even a bit sloppy. A casual attitude toward matching action and spatial configuration from shot to shot obtained from his earliest shorts with Laurel and Hardy, when that attitude was widely shared, through his features of the 1930s and 1940s, when a stricter continuity reined. Minor "cheat cuts" are frequent in McCarey, and even outright mismatches occur regularly, as in the courtroom scene in *The Awful Truth*, where Cary Grant is seated in one shot and standing in the next. Fundamental to McCarey's technique is the axial cut, a shift from one shot to another with no change in angle, usually from a long to a medium scale. This practice was also in wide use in the late silent period but generally disfavored in the sound era, when a cut without a change in angle was supposed to draw attention to itself and thereby threaten the "invisible" editing that was increasingly favored in the studio system.

Though as unassuming as most of his other stylistic predilections, McCarey's continued use of this technique does give his work a restless air even at its most placid or subdued, as in *Going My Way* or *The Bells of St. Mary's*. Often, in his films of the 1930s, the elastic conception of space conveyed by the editing patterns creates the most pungent comic effects. In *Ruggles of Red Gap*, for instance, when the staid and proper butler encounters his new uncouth employers, his horrified recoil from their rustic ways is registered through a wildly mismatched cut, from a medium shot of all the characters present to a reverse-angle that shows the butler suddenly at a much exaggerated distance, impossible for him to have traversed in the split-second of the edit. This scrappy, slightly messy quality of the editing—from which an admirer of McCarey like Jean Renoir might have learned a thing or two—makes the films' rhythms bracingly unpredictable and gives an off-center edge to narrative emphases. Typically, McCarey refrains from accentuating what most other directors would highlight and often lingers over what they would hurry past, efface, or ignore. The fire that consumes the church at the end of *Going My Way* would serve as a dramatic high point in another director's work, but McCarey practically brushes it off. Almost never does he rely upon editing to confer conventional emphases on the material. Close-ups are surprisingly rare, point-of-view shots virtually nonexistent; in *Six of a Kind,* the only point-of-view shot in the whole film, and one of the few in the entirety of the director's work, is given to a dog who suddenly sees something to chase. McCarey's default mode is what the French called the *plan américain*, a medium-shot of one or more characters. Wood argues that this type of shot showing two characters is the fundamental feature of McCareyian style: Granting the two figures equal weight in the visual dynamic, says Wood, it expresses a principle of democracy that becomes, in McCarey's work, an aesthetic principle as well. Reaction shots, when they appear, are often curiously displaced. In *Good Sam*, for example, the title character arrives home bent on a romantic interlude with his wife; neither he nor we know that two grumpy neighbors have come over to pick a bone with him, and Sam, in his ardor, is deaf to his wife's efforts to alert him. As he escalates their intimacies, McCarey cuts away to close-ups of the sour-pussed couple, looking on disapprovingly. No shot has established the couple's presence, and they are not shown in the same shot as Sam and Lucy until the end of the scene, so we have no idea where they are in the room, giving the shots a comically disjunctive charge. Though rarely used for purposes of rhetorical punctuation, McCarey's editing brings a quality of discord to his work that seldom abates.

McCarey collaborated with the cinematographer Gregg Toland on *The Kid from Spain* in 1931, ten years before Toland shot *Citizen Kane*. In his work with McCarey, Toland undertook some of his earliest experiments with long takes and depth-of-field, the techniques made famous in his collaboration with Welles. In an especially striking example, a gun-toting villain boasts that he can plug the Kid (Eddie Cantor) at any distance, and the Kid tests him by running into the distance and turning back to shout, "Could you hit me here?" With the hapless villain hulking in the foreground, he repeats this taunt again and again as he moves farther and farther into the background while remaining in clear focus, until he disappears into the frame's vanishing point. Another instance, in the number "In the Moonlight," features a long take that tracks laterally to follow Cantor, with surprising elements popping into the frame, arrayed fancifully from foreground to background, in synch with the lyrics Cantor sings.

These examples evince a stylistic bravura largely forsaken in McCarey's subsequent work, but he retains a malleable sense of the film frame that derives from these early influences much as his cutting style has its roots in the late silent period. In general, McCarey's shots are longer in duration than the Classical Hollywood norm; the main reason he is not ordinarily grouped with cinematic masters of the long take like Murnau, Ophuls, Wyler, Welles, or Minnelli is that his penchant for extended shots is not embellished with dramatic movement of the camera, as it often is in those filmmakers' work. A typical McCarey effect turns on a minute shift, a slight reframing or brief, sudden pan. In *The Milky Way*, a long take shows a con artist (Adolphe Menjou) trying to dupe a naif (Harold Lloyd) with flattery. In the left periphery of the frame hangs a painting of a distinguished-looking gentleman, seemingly a mere background adornment, with no relevance to the action. Suddenly, the con man indicates it with a fatuous compliment, assuming it to be a portrait of the naif's father. "That was here when we moved in," Lloyd replies. "It could be *your* father. And that"—the camera quickly pans slightly to the left, revealing a previously unseen portrait of an elderly woman hanging on the wall right beside the first one—"could be your mother!"

For its deflation of the con man's pretense, the joke depends on a small, precise gesture, a swift, lithe movement of the camera. The same kind of technique abets some of McCarey's most intense moments of pathos. In *Love Affair*, for example, Michel discovers Terry's handicap when he sees one of his paintings hanging on the wall of her bedroom, knowing that it was given to a woman who could not walk. The revelation is remarkable in its restraint: We see Michel in a medium-long shot, facing the camera, struck dumb by what he sees off-screen. With a slight move to the left, the camera discloses the painting, hanging on the opposite wall, reflected in the mirror beside him, fixes on it only for an instant, then moves back to Michel, holding on him as he silently parses the momentous significance of what he has discovered. The shot gains its piercing reticence in the slightness of the gesture, gracefully avoiding the punctuation of a reverse-shot to reveal the painting. The effect is heightened because it rhymes with an earlier shot in the film: As Terry stands on a balcony anticipating her reunion with Michel at the Empire State Building, she gazes beyond the camera as a glass door slowly swings open beside her, reflecting the reverse-field of the camera's perspective and bringing into view the image of the very building where they are destined to meet—and fated not to.

Due to its warmth and earthiness, few would call McCarey's work austere, but his style depends on an absence of conventional inflection with affinities to the cinema's great minimalists, from Carl Dreyer to Yasujiro Ozu—who is said to have modeled his masterpiece, *Tokyo Story* (1953), on McCarey's *Make Way for Tomorrow*. This point is illustrated in McCarey's typical handling of the scene as a basic dramatic unit. Variations in rhythm are carefully managed within a small range, but the leisurely pacing remains quite constant and always portends the possibility, at least by Hollywood's standards, of a certain listlessness in the treatment—a prospect yet furthered by the long takes, fixed camera setups, and predominant abstention from using editing to punctuate action. But tendencies like these run even deeper in McCarey's work. What makes the last scene of *Make Way for Tomorrow* so devastating, for instance, is how straightforwardly, even starkly, it is presented. The husband and wife are parting as he boards a train; they will probably never see each other again. He gets on the train, and not only does the camera remain with the wife on the platform, it never cuts to the husband again. In a lax long shot, we can see him take his seat if we happen to look, and as the train pulls away, we might be able to glimpse his profile through a window, but he is as lost to us as he is to her. The camera does not shift to assist our view. The heated underscoring that accompanied such pathos-riddled railway leave-takings since the movies began makes no appearance here. A few bars of slow music murmur on the soundtrack—"Let Me Call You Sweetheart," the song the couple sang together—but the shots are simply modulated, uninsistent. A cut to the wife in a medium close-up shows her sadly watching as the train departs—the anticipated reverse-shot to her husband never does come—and then, just as she starts to turn away, the shot fades and the film ends.

McCarey's largely uninflected treatment comes off as bracing understatement at such dramatic heights and a welcome antidote to sentimentality on those occasions when the drama seems unearned. It lends itself especially well to scenes of religious content like the chapel interlude in *Love Affair*, though such scenes are surprisingly rare in McCarey's work; or episodes of oratorical elevation—which are legion, from Ruggles's passionate delivery of the Gettysburg Address in *Ruggles of Red Gap* to the recitations of the American "Pledge of Allegiance" in *Once Upon a Honeymoon* and *The Bells of St. Mary's* or John's address to his alma mater at the end of *My Son John*. The exquisite last scene of *The Bells of St. Mary's* achieves an almost Dreyeresque intensity with its sparse means—a held shot, a small shift of light. An earthy yet saintly nun (Ingrid Bergman) is being sent away from her church to convalesce for tuberculosis, and because she has not been told the reason for her relocation, she is saddened and bitter. A dim, low-angled shot from a sideward vantage shows a staircase for many seconds before she descends it, and holds on it for many seconds after she has left, as if to convey in this lingering a sanctified aura of the space Sister Benedict has passed through. At the last minute, the church's pastor (Bing

Crosby) relents and tells her why she must leave; a close-up shows her face tilting into light as she looks up at him with an expression of joy. (In what other director's work does the news that one is suffering from tuberculosis elicit joy?) The pastor watches her go, and the reverse-angle is held on the delicately illumined courtyard after she has left it. As with the absence of the reverse-shot in *Make Way for Tomorrow*, the return to the shot of the pastor that most directors would count on to bring closure never appears, and the film ends on a note of breathless suspension.

Indirection, anticipation, suspension (as opposed to ordinary "suspense")—these are constructs that recur constantly in McCarey's work, the contours that give unexpected shadings to scenes from which ordinary inflections have been withheld. The general tenor of a McCarey scene is searching, not knowing—unlike the razor-sharp construction of a typical scene by Billy Wilder, say, where everything snaps into its predetermined place, and though McCarey's scenes are often emotionally detailed, they are usually too self-contained to be called intricate. As a comic artist McCarey is more drawn to the passing glance than to the running gag. A scene from *The Milky Way* illustrates the point: Hectoring him about his indecent and unlikely involvement in the boxing game, Harold Lloyd's sweetheart sits down on his hat, and when she stands up the rim clings to her bottom as she stalks indignantly away. The sitting-on-the-hat gag was already well worn by 1936; indeed, McCarey had made liberal use of it himself, including just two years before in *Six of a Kind*. Another director would likely have made the revelation of the hat's sticking to the posterior the springboard to a running gag, on the order of the sequence in *Bringing Up Baby* where Katharine Hepburn's dress rips down the back in public and Cary Grant has to go to preposterous lengths to conceal the tear in a mounting series of comic riffs. For McCarey, the sitting-on-the-hat is itself the joke, with the hat clinging to the rear just a punch line, an end point. It is a variant on McCarey's beloved fart-at-the-dinner table bit, with the humor deriving from Lloyd's awkward attempts to soft-pedal the gaffe, gesturing ineffectually and tilting his head feebly to catch a glimpse of the crushed hat as the oblivious sweetheart prattles on. Once she stalks off, a joke that could have built much further is curtly curtailed, and the hat is never heard of again.

McCarey's gags can play as riffs in the sense that they often seem to come out of nowhere; the most solemn of his scenes might contain a sudden, passing gag, like the glimpse of a little girl taking an appraising gander at the church's benefactor during a mass in *The Bells of St. Mary's*. But they don't tend to build in the usual sense; more often, they are tossed off as the scene veers away in search of a next one. Even when the gags are repetitive, they tend to spring up as singular events rather than links in a comic chain a la Chaplin or Keaton. Laurel and Hardy's jokes all boil down to the same premise: Laurel's goofs trigger Hardy's bluster again and again. What McCarey famously contributed to the duo's antics was to slow them down, retarding Laurel's already languid double-takes and making Hardy's epic slow-burns even more dilatory. McCarey's comedy of delayed reaction, even of *non*-reaction (i.e., the fart at the dinner table), made him an ideal director for players like Groucho Marx and Mae West, both of whom practiced a form of verbal comedy that depended on their outré but nonchalant utterances being received by interlocutors rendered too shocked, baffled, or otherwise nonplused to respond. Marx's barbed witticisms assault reason by turning it against itself; they are relentless yet fleeting in the sense that each is tossed off in a trice, trenchant in form but off-handed in delivery, requiring that listeners be disarmed so the barrage can continue, and drawing anyone who dares to reply into their own twisted logic. With his clipped, sing-song intonations, Groucho Marx could be said to do at the level of the line what McCarey does at the level of the scene.

Deferral and frustration figure in much comedy, but McCarey takes these elements further than most, weaving them deeply into temporal structures of scenes and larger narrative forms. When his characteristic refusal to mark ordinary "beats" or turns of scenes—a refusal, as it were, to "direct" audiences' responses to the material—is combined with a distention of action, a very particular kind of cinematic pleasure results, with a decided bent toward *un*-pleasure. In literal terms, many of the stars McCarey worked with in his earliest work—Laurel and Hardy, the Marx Brothers, Eddie Cantor—all forged comic personae based on being annoying. However endearing they may have turned out to be in the longer run, their jokes depended in the first instance on provoking irritation. What McCarey did for the most part in his work with them was to make them even more annoying—by, for instance, slowing down Laurel and Hardy and prolonging our exposure to their excruciating travails. According to Stanley Cavell, one learns in McCarey's work to look for the disturbing subtext beneath a seemingly agreeable surface. McCarey, says Cavell, "has the power to walk a scene right up to that verge where the comic is no longer comic, without either losing the humor or letting the humor deny the humanity of its victims."[1] In this he stands as a crucial forerunner of contemporary cringe comedy.

Among McCarey's favorite jokes is another variation on the fart at the dinner table, in which one party pours liquid into another's lap or onto another's rump—inadvertently, when an aimed-for cup shifts place, as in the Laurel and Hardy short *We Faw Down* (1928), or deliberately, as in the Max Davison short *Pass the Gravy* (1928), when a malicious boy douses his father with a garden hose. Versions of the gag litter McCarey's early work, always depending on a lag in the recipient's reaction that allows the deluge to proceed much longer than seems natural. This over-extension itself *is* the joke, one that McCarey seems never to tire of. In his early sound comedies, many scenes derive humor from the simple fact of being prolonged, without significant variation or development. Eddie Cantor's protracted encounter with an irate border guard in *The Kid from Spain*, Mary Boland's extended sojourn on a cliff-side limb in *Six of a Kind*, even the scene where Irene Dunne crashes the party in *The Awful Truth* all qualify as examples in which the very duration of the scene is meant to be the funny part.

Even after 1937, as the comedy gradually receded into the background, eclipsed by more "serious" overtones, the too-long scene remains a staple of McCarey's oeuvre. The last scene of *Love Affair* is an obvious example, but cases in which these scenes crop up along the way, stalling the narrative momentum, are even more instructive, like Ginger Rogers's encounter with the counterspy (Albert Dekker) in *Once Upon a Honeymoon* or the scene on the bus near the start of *Good Sam*. The first of these comes at a narrative turning point, suggesting that it must set up further complications to be developed later, but the counterspy is dispensed with quickly (and with shocking violence), amplifying in retrospect the scene's digressive aspect. Similarly, the scene on the bus goes on so long that it should by rights, according to every edict of the Classical Hollywood model, lay groundwork for further development. Instead, none of the scene's characters or events is ever referred to again.

Nor can such examples be accounted for as directorial slackening since versions of them appear very early, and they are so much a part of the fabric and feeling of the work, and of such odd interest and unusual coloring in themselves. Indeed, many of these seeming digressions, like the Christmas pageant in *The Bells of St. Mary's*, stand among McCarey's greatest sequences; the strange rhythms they impart, the ineffable shifts of tone and mood, whether barely perceptible or boldly clashing, attest strongly to McCarey's commitment to an aesthetic of the spontaneous, his willingness to pursue narrative lines without conventional payoffs. Far from being extraneous, they point to some of his central concerns; the sense of excruciation they often produce is perhaps the most pressing and pervasive affect of his work as a whole.

The stock Hollywood villain has no place in a McCarey film, mainly because the films have so little interest in the dynamics of power. The figure of the evil banker, already a platitude on the appearance of Gatewood (Berton Churchill) in *Stagecoach* (1939) or Potter (Lionel Barrymore) in *It's a Wonderful Life* (1946), is inconceivable in a McCarey film. The closest he comes are two figures in the parish films, either of which could easily have been portrayed as evil antagonists. In *Going My Way*, the banker who holds the deed on the church is played with a genial air (by Gene Lockhart) even as he threatens to foreclose, and he is shown from the start to have a loving relationship to his grown son (James Brown). In *The Bells of St. Mary's*, the industrialist who wants to raze the parish school to make way for a parking lot is no heartless titan but an anxious, put-upon softy, played by the loveable character actor Henry Travers, who specialized in sweetly ineffectual types like the father in *Shadow of a Doubt* (1943) and went on to play the angel in *It's a Wonderful Life* the next year. When these characters inevitably see the errors of their ways, the turn is not a Scrooge-like conversion but a simple fulfillment of their better natures. In the terms of these films, both merely need to see *themselves* anew.

The benign suspension of judgment that conditions the treatment of these figures extends to nearly all of McCarey's characters. Even the Fascist baron in *Once Upon a Honeymoon* is no snarling Nazi like Conrad Veidt in *Casablanca* (1942); one of the achievements of that peculiar film is to lay bare the odium beneath the baron's urbane manner without relinquishing the humaneness that pervades the whole. Even the selfishness and cruelty of Bark and Lucy's children in *Make Way for Tomorrow* is tempered a bit by a final scene in which they reflect remorsefully on what they have done. Both of the parish films feature characters who are prostitutes, depicted with a startling kindness and matter-of-fact acknowledgment of the realities of their plight, a representation entirely free of the usual lurid sensationalism or whore-with-a-heart-of-gold sentimentality. A sense of acceptance pervades McCarey's films overall, a spirit of generosity that recalls the work of his admirer Renoir.

The Awful Truth provides an especially telling lens upon McCarey's work because much of the film seems alien to the dominant spirit of his work. The film stands alongside *It Happened One Night* (1934), *Nothing Sacred* (1934), *My Man Godfrey* (1936), *Theodora Goes Wild* (1936), *Bringing*

Up Baby, and *His Girl Friday* (1940) among the quintessential "screwball" films—a 1930s cycle of romantic comedies based on the unlikely pairings of seemingly antagonistic couples, with plots spurred by impulsive motivations, dialogue marked by a bristling quicksilver wit, and occasional bouts of punchy slapstick. By comparison with an example like *His Girl Friday*—famous for its breakneck pace and the rapidity of its dialogue—*The Awful Truth* is downright sluggish, but by contrast with McCarey's most characteristic work it moves, for much of its duration, at lightning speed. A significant part of the cycle is made up of Cavellian comedies of remarriage, tales of divorcing couples who realize in the end that they belong together after all. McCarey prefigured the template in a film like *Indiscreet*, and it is certainly hospitable to his recurrent interest in alienated couples.

Yet *The Awful Truth* is the only one of McCarey's films in the last twenty-five years of his career, excepting *Rally Round the Flag, Boys!*, that could be called a straight-on comedy at all, though all have significant doses of humor. Indeed, its comedy is sharply etched, its punchlines hit swiftly and surely, at least in its first two-thirds. Most commonly—and always, from this point on—McCarey's plots progress with an unhurried, tentative movement. The funniest scene in *The Awful Truth* finds Lucy (Irene Dunne) crashing a society party disguised as the manic, loopy sister of her estranged husband Jerry (Cary Grant) in an effort to sabotage his romance with an heiress. The scene is pure McCarey, as the humor derives less from a sequence of surefire "gags" than from the impromptu quality of the whole put-on. Not for the first time, Jerry sees Lucy anew, perceives—and is moved by—something of the desperation just beneath her act, and even gets into the spirit of it, playing along, however passive-aggressively. Then, on a lark, the two take off together, suddenly speeding along in Jerry's car, bickering haplessly over the still-blaring radio, until the police pull them over. They spar Laurel-and-Hardy-style with the blustery officers for a capricious while, when Lucy takes it into her head to wreck the car. The police turn instantly solicitous and agree to spirit them away to a mountain cabin that pops up as if pulled out of a magician's hat, and Lucy and Jerry sojourn there at some length, lolling in adjacent rooms, their awareness of how they have hurt each other hanging in the air like the curtain between the lovers' beds in *It Happened One Night*, until the inevitable makeshift reconciliation.

In this last stretch a classic screwball comedy shifts on a dime into a Leo McCarey film. Though definite, the move is graceful enough that one might not be able to sense much of a difference. The slowing of the action, the turn to a halting, exploratory advance just when things are supposed to be snapping together and wrapping up, the hovering sense of anticipation—these are far from the stuff of the whiz-bang resolutions favored by the Classical Hollywood model. Lucy and Jerry's reunion is scarcely in doubt, all but decreed by the genre, but the deferred route the film takes gives it a bittersweet cast, and we are deprived of the proverbial satisfaction of a final view of the lovers' affirming embrace. In the same stroke the film makes a joke of its own terminal protraction, repeatedly diverting the viewer's gaze to shots of a cuckoo clock with uncannily live figurines in Alpine garb emerging from side-by-side double-doors and performing languid jigs to mark the passing time. Rather than the final kiss of *Bringing Up Baby* and countless others, *The Awful Truth* displaces the view of the reunion with a final shot of the clock to signify what is happening off-screen, with the male figure slyly doing a slow-motion pirouette to saunter after his female counterpart inside of her door.

If not for the comedy-of-remarriage cycle, McCarey might have found no footing in the screwball genre at all, despite his close associations with it. Staples of the form include the obligatory "meet cute" of the future couple and a central conceit that provides a through-line to offset the films' putatively freewheeling structures—a shared journey in *It Happened One Night*, a chase after a domesticated leopard with a purloined bone in *Bringing Up Baby*, a quest for a journalistic scoop on a hot story in *His Girl Friday*. In most cases McCarey's couples are already paired when we first encounter them, and if they *do* "meet cute," as in *Love Affair* and its remake, they are soon parted. The marriage plot that furnishes so much grist for Hollywood's mill figures hardly at all in McCarey's corpus except as a target of derision (in the Laurel and Hardy shorts or the Marx Brothers feature *Duck Soup*). So resistant is McCarey to the tight causality typical of Classical Hollywood structure that he seeks refuge from it again and again in episodic plots that enable digressive, often arbitrary turns. Many comedies of remarriage supply their divided couples with new potential partners who serve as rivals and foils, but *The Awful Truth* crowds in several such figures, treated in sequence, amplifying the spotty progression of the story throughout that comes to the fore in the end.

McCarey's muted, uninflected treatment of the scene as a dramatic unit sometimes confers a kind of stranded quality. One of the most painful scenes in *Make Way for Tomorrow* shows an elderly mother telling her grown son a "little secret," just "between us two": "You were always my favorite child." In another kind of film this exchange might have provided a moment of inspirational uplift as a simple expression of maternal affection. Even amid the tender anguish of McCarey's famously harrowing film, some of that feeling comes through. What makes the scene really piercing, though, is that the mother means to spare the son the task of informing her that she is no longer welcome to live with his family and must go to a nursing home. Having gleaned this plan, she lets him off the hook by pretending that the idea of leaving is her own and feigning anticipation of her new life in the home. We see that the son fully understands what she is doing, and that she knows he knows, but neither can speak of it. The scene has a clear emotional trajectory, yet its rhythms do not follow ordinary "beats." There's no point at which one could locate the turns of feeling; instead, the scene proceeds with a certain quiet inertia, giving it a rawness and intimacy that make it more devastating than a conventionally emphasized rendering.

The last scene of McCarey's subsequent film, *Love Affair*, is instructive to place beside this one. After a whirlwind shipboard romance, Terry (Irene Dunne) and Michel (Charles Boyer) pledge to meet again in six months, having worked through their various entanglements and determined whether they have both gained a sufficient degree of freedom and responsibility to commit to each other. In route to this rendezvous, Terry is hit by a car and rendered unable to walk. She resolves to let Michel believe she has forgotten him rather than risk burdening him or becoming the object of his pity. Michel, meanwhile, is heartbroken by her failure to appear. Time passes as Michel becomes an accomplished painter and Terry a music teacher in a children's school, until they happen to meet in public one day. On this encounter Terry conceals her handicap, but afterward, Michel shows up at her apartment, presumably to confront her about her perceived rejection. The final scene is a long, awkward dialogue as Terry reclines on a sofa while Michel paces restlessly around the room, his demeanor shifting from impatience to perplexity to passive-aggressive reticence. To his annoyance, Terry responds with nothing but chipper, imperturbable conviviality. Michel's conclusive discovery of Terry's condition may be the stuff of movie romance climaxes, but McCarey fades to black almost as soon as that revelation is achieved. The crux of the scene is its deferral. The scene is a seemingly interminable interlude of excruciation, fraught with dramatic irony yet so down-tempo, so unhurried, that it gives no inkling of a conclusion lurking anywhere nearby.

As in many of McCarey's films the plot turns on passivity, the very opposite of the usual principles that drive more conventional narratives. In *Make Way for Tomorrow*, why do Lucy and Bark, no matter what the circumstances, so submissively allow themselves to be separated? Why do Terry and Michel delay their union or, when they form their perverse compact to part company before wedding, give any thought at all to questions of responsibility—exactly the kind of stuffy consideration the Hollywood romance usually demands be swept aside? In *The Awful Truth*, the main characters slide resignedly into divorce, more as a default option than a decisive choice, and the whole point is that neither really wants to separate. *Ruggles of Red Gap* is about a servant whose role entails compliance by definition, while *Going My Way* and *The Bells of St. Mary's* concern priests and nuns who have pledged their lives to the church, with significant plot points turning on their being moved involuntarily from parish to parish.

The final scene of *Love Affair* is built around Terry's immobility, an unpromising basis for a climactic moment. The viewer knows she cannot stand but Michel does not; the drama resides in his shifting reactions to the fact that she does not rise from her position on the couch. He extends his arms as if to help her up and seems vaguely taken aback when she remains seated, doubtfully bending instead to kiss her hands, as if saving face in answer to her refusal. Their conversation turns on Michel's conceit that he was the one who failed to keep their assignation, a premise Terry pretends to accept. But when does she realize he is not telling the truth? At what point does he begin to suspect that her immobility hides a deeper secret? As in the scene in *Make Way for Tomorrow*, the core of the scene is implicit, unspoken, the encounters painfully mutual in the play of knowing and unknowing. In a passing grace note, McCarey places the camera behind Terry, so that we see her for an instant in the same position in which Michel has painted her, but the shot is casual, and we have only seen the painting previously in an off-handed, sideward glimpse. When we see it straight on at the end of this scene, the grace note may take on an added resonance in retrospect, but that's just the point. Registers of thought and feeling in the scene are constantly shifting, but though this sense of flux is felt pervasively, the exact moments, the wheres and the whens that a more conventional dramaturge would pinpoint, remain elusive.

In the absence of characters who act decisively rather than being acted upon, McCarey's plots for the most part lack the kinds of conflicts most narratives thrive on, introducing a certain lassitude (perhaps akin to the one Rivette discovers in Hawks) that is key to the films' gentleness. As the examples above indicate, however, a drama of will is never far from the surface. Even the most seemingly passive of McCarey's characters must take their stands, however these moments may involve a resolution *not* to do something—the mother's determination not to cause her son pain and Terry's resolve to live her life alone, allowing Michel to think she does not love him rather than reveal her disability. These assertions of will are quite stunningly obstinate, even though what they reveal is a most profound denial of the self.

Film rouge and the politics of authorship

My Son John marks a turn in McCarey's career toward a model of social-consciousness cinema deriving from a heightened conviction about the dangers posed by Communism to American democracy. Among the first witnesses in the initial Hollywood HUAC hearings of October 1947, McCarey stated decisively in that forum that he personally knew of many American Communists in the film industry, mostly among the writers, and believed that they had indeed been inserting propaganda into American movies. When asked whether Hollywood should dedicate itself to making anti-Communist movies to counter this danger, however, McCarey demurred on the grounds that movies were an art form that could only be corrupted by the intrusion of politics. For Hollywood to make anti-Communist films, according to McCarey, would be tantamount to the same thing he thought the Soviets were doing. It is therefore surprising to find McCarey making exactly such a film only a few years later, though it is equally clear that his decision to make the film grew out of the same sincere and intense (however misguided) social commitment that his HUAC testimony reflected. As a document of the Cold War, *My Son John* is endlessly fascinating. It bespeaks something of the "consensus" ideology of the time that reads very differently now. At the same time, it is unmistakably a

"Leo McCarey film." This complicated overlap is what makes it such a suggestive test case.

The film opens on a long shot of a residential street in late fall or winter. The trees are bare, stray leaves scattered across the lawns. The houses are large, in craftsman and colonial designs—the kind of street meant to read as nondescript in an ordinary establishing shot from a Hollywood film of the 1950s. We might be about to see a chapter in the life of Andy Hardy, an episode of bumptious Americana, or a more sober account of the daily travails of a Man in a Gray Flannel Suit. The setting could be a nascent suburb, though it lacks the hilly expanses of the neighborhood where Mr. Blandings built his dream house in the 1948 film of that name, the winding roads with sun-blanched pavement of Hummingbird Hill in *Sitting Pretty* (1948), or the spacious Cape Cods of *Miracle on 34th Street* (1947)—all definitive portraits of American suburbia as it made its way into movies after the Second World War. More likely it is meant to stand for small-town America, the houses placed squarely shoulder to shoulder, spaced enough apart to afford just the proper degree of privacy, with the comfort, serenity, and homogeneity that all of this implies.

It will turn out that the film has a vested interest in obscuring its locale. Late in the film Washington DC makes a picturesque appearance, with all the well-known signifiers of that location in place, when Lucille (Helen Hayes), the would-be matriarch of the Jefferson clan, goes there to investigate the doings of her wayward son. She travels by airplane in the first flight of her life, and some express concern that she wants to go "up" there while others, on her return, are surprised that she has gone "down" there. Thus, we know that this place we see in the opening shot is at a considerable distance (thus the need to travel by plane) from the national capitol, north *and* south. Slip-knots of this sort are readily accommodated by the virtual world of the cinema and its attendant logics, which often require them. The Jefferson hometown is "Anywhere U.S.A." (just the phrase the script uses to describe it, in fact), of a sort well known to viewers of Hollywood movies, a

Deleuzean "any-space-whatever," a figment rendered ordinary to translate a given milieu into a theoretically generalized "middle-class" and, with this appearance of familiarity, to aid in reinforcing whatever norms happen to be on the docket. But the strangeness of cinema, heralded by the auteurists as a force that could unexpectedly counter even the most hidebound regimes, is hard to keep at bay. Something is off here. The bare trees and gray skies cast an autumnal melancholy over the image, and the church bells that ring confer a correspondingly funereal air. The opening shot is held long past the demands of the usual "content curve," the point at which the viewer has presumably assimilated the information of a given shot. It is one of McCarey's too-long strophes, unassumingly placed right at the start of the film. Two young men in military garb toss a football as an older man, their father (Dean Jagger), comes out on the porch. A next-door neighbor hollers a convivial yet impertinent gibe about the noise, while the sons humorously chide the father about his own maladroit bearing in the matter of athletics. He blusters mildly in response and turns his attention to the matter of Lucille, his wife, who is keeping them all waiting again. All of this is viewed from a fixed vantage, as if to acknowledge that the unfolding action is so familiar that we can take it in from a distance—voices absorbed in the eerily resonant ambient soundscape, and audible only with effort. What we know is that this is a family of sporty and energetic sons with ties to the army and a father who is somewhat out of step, a world where teasing is not uncommon.

Over the first few scenes we see what appears to be an ordinary round of activity on an average Sunday: a good-natured scramble to get to church, a peaceful interlude at the mass, the gradual settling-down to a hearty Sunday dinner, the teasing unabated all the while. Despite concerns over their mother's nervousness, Ben and Chuck rib her with boys-will-be-boys abandon, in a way that might seem disconcertingly flirtatious if we were not supposed to know better. Other off-notes, too, persist. Sitting between her sons in church,

Lucille bows too ardently in prayer and the boys exchange a wary glance over her head. A third son has not arrived for dinner, though whether this absence denotes a simple lapse or a covert refusal is not clear. What makes it sting especially, though, is that this is no ordinary Sunday, as we have come to understand. What gives the proceedings their pervading sense of unease is that the brothers of the truant son are about to be shipped off that afternoon for combat in the Korean War. Boyishly incorrigible, they promise to send Lucille an opium pipe from the Orient. The church pastor comes to usher the boys off, and Lucille, in another too-long stroke, leans into the car that will bear them away for overextended good-bye kisses as her husband tries feebly to restrain her. In short order the doctor appears with a vial of pills for Lucille's "nerves," prescribing three a day. She scoffs at the idea, but just as she accepted the wine she first refused when her husband plied her with it at dinner, she finally assents to this pacifier too. Alone in the kitchen, though, she stows the pills away, in a gesture of secret defiance.

The errant child turns into the prodigal son when he finally does appear for his first visit in over a year, in the welter of Lucille's unbridled joy and Dan's stiffly affectionate welcome. Both parents feel neglected, clearly, but Lucille tries to indulge the son's caprices while Dan resents the hints of disrespect. For his part, John (Robert Walker) conveys an affection so guarded, so spotted with shades of potential condescension, that his parents can hardly be blamed for suspecting that it is false. The disquieting core of the film tracks John's erratic comings and goings as these unspoken suspicions fester. No sooner has he arrived than he runs off to meet his old professor and mentor from the "teacher's college," a "highbrow" type in Dan's jaundiced estimation. John boldly red-pencils the text of his father's planned speech to the American Legion instead of flattering and rubber-stamping it as expected and hoped. The off-notes proliferate unnervingly until Lucille herself takes note of them. She and Dan both remark that John seems "different," "nervous," that something is "the matter." He's just a little tired, John replies, that's all. Lucille confides in him her worry that "I have a feeling we're not as *close* as we were." He affably dismisses her concerns.

So unsettled and distracted is the father by his son's visit and his perceived slights that Dan starts to harangue Lucille about it while driving and causes a minor accident, rearing another motorist's car in mid-rant. The incident is treated with the mild whimsy of an innocuous sitcom of the day, but when Stedman (Van Heflin), the man whose car has been hit, shows up at the house to collect on a bill for repairs, Lucille's suspicions are further aroused, especially when Stedman abandons his demand for reimbursement too easily and John, hearing of the visit, expresses a vaguely acrid and unaccountable interest in it. Her hunches are not misplaced: It is soon revealed that Stedman is really an FBI agent investigating Communist infiltration. The very next day Dan brandishes a newspaper headline announcing that a "girl" named Ruth Carlin has been "accused of treason" for Communist ties. All the while John keeps popping in and out, still maddeningly impervious in his way as the rumors swirl. Still, he continues to reassure his parents, even acquiescing to swear on a Bible. In a clumsy showdown, Dan confronts John once and for all, impulsively clunking him on the head with that same Bible and pushing him over a table for good measure.

Still, when John departs for good the next day, Lucille still has faith in him, however shaken. "Remember you are my tomorrows," she says, and a quick, portentous chord of music on the soundtrack, and his own fazed pause, indicates that this is the first of her gambits that has really gotten to him. He goes off nonetheless, but he has left something behind, a mysterious key, and when he places a call to reclaim it, Lucille takes the sudden initiative to jet off to Washington, without consultation with her husband. There she pays an enervated visit to John at his government office, then—observed by the FBI all the while—she heads wearily to the disgraced Ruth Carlin's apartment where she confirms her worst fears when she discovers that the key fits the door's lock. This Hitchcockian turn is the last straw. Back home, Lucille sinks into despond, John reappears out of nowhere in an effort to mollify her one last time—though with a demonic edge that seems, while still slight, now quite distinct, nearly unmistakable—and Stedman lives up to his name in remaining steadfast in his conviction of John's guilt. As a distraught Lucille is tended off screen by her stand-by phalanx of doctors and priests, John creeps through hallways, flees up stairways, and escapes through windows like a film noir heavy. Despite these seeming retreats, we discover John yet again, surprisingly, back inside the house, standing at the foot of the stairs overhearing the hushed ministrations above—his mother's pitiful supplications and the answering recitation of the "Lord's Prayer"—with an expression both fiendish and oddly beatific. Thereupon he withdraws one last time back to Washington, where he makes a hasty tape recording of his final testament, reconsiders a flight to Lisbon and phones Stedman to turn himself in, but is waylaid, as he rushes to surrender, by a speeding sedan whose shadowy occupants riddle his car with machine-gun bullets, causing it to career and overturn, coming to rest on its side on the steps of the Lincoln Memorial. Stedman quickly materializes, looking down through a shattered window to witness John's dying words, a last-gasp request that his recording be played at his alma-mater's commencement ceremony, where he had been slated to speak. In the final scene, we hear the whole of this address, an unequivocal repudiation of Communism as a fraudulent ideology mired in mind-control, and a pious affirmation of parental and godly authority, emanating from an altar at the front of a church-like hall in a shaft of heavenly light to the accompaniment of an angelic chorus on the soundtrack as rows of fresh-faced graduates listen raptly.

In this final stretch, a film that has become increasingly unhinged goes entirely off the rails. But where, in all this, is Leo McCarey? An unreconstructed auteurist could viably answer: everywhere. Even the social-consciousness angle has a precedent if we read *Make Way for Tomorrow* as a Depression-era cautionary tale on the treatment of the elderly. For the rest,

McCarey's signatures are all present and accounted for. The characteristic narrative rhythms, the loose editing patterns and unmatched shots, the withdrawn virtuosity combined with an overweening sense of confident modesty, the too-long scenes and the quick grace-notes, the lag-and-lurch, the uninflected treatment of the scene as a dramatic unit, the relative indifference to overall coherence, the imperceptible blending of tones and abruptly colliding affects, the preference for complication and irresolution and the unexpected turn—all figure in *My Son John* from beginning to problematic end. Indeed, the status of *My Son John* as something of a "problem" picture is just what makes it such an evocative case. An important task of auteurism was to rescue such "problem" films from unjust devaluation. Despite recent attempts, *My Son John* remains resistant to such recuperation, so instead of busying ourselves with lost causes we can turn our attentions to the dynamics of "failure" in the light of auteurism. What happens when a film *cannot* be repatriated into the canon, even when it shares crucial features with those that have been? What could this tell us about the cultural politics of auteurism?

The "problem" in question is precisely the politics of anti-Communism. *My Son John* is one of a cycle of anti-Communist films made in Hollywood beginning in 1948 as expiation, implicitly or explicitly, for the alleged "injection" of Communist propaganda. About thirty appeared in total, with a critical mass of titles released between the late 1940s and mid-1950s, but continuing sporadically to 1962. Forming a quasi-genre that one could archly call "film rouge," in honor of its overlap with film noir, the cycle is as disreputable as any in American movies, having attracted strikingly little critical attention. A voluminous literature exists on Cold War culture, but studies of HUAC and Hollywood are often limited by disciplinary rifts. The best-known works in the field, such as Victor Navasky's *Naming Names* or Ceplair and Englund's *The Inquisition in Hollywood*, are serviceable on the social and historical contexts, but have little interest in placing the films themselves in those contexts. Important exceptions include work by Thom Andersen and

Michael Rogin, both dating from the twilight of the Cold War and both bringing to bear on their discussions as much knowledge of and interest in cinema as of the political contexts. Andersen's piece "Red Hollywood" was first published in 1985 and developed into an invaluable essay film of the same title ten years later in collaboration with Noël Burch. Andersen's essay scrutinizes thoroughly the literature on HUAC, Hollywood, and the blacklist before proceeding to an illuminating survey of films made by blacklisted directors in a quasi-genre Andersen dubs "film gris" due to its intersection with noir (inspiring my own coinage of film rouge). Like noir itself, film gris yields a panoply of filmmakers with obvious prestige among its filmographies, including certified auteurs like Nicholas Ray, Joseph Losey, and Jules Dassin alongside enterprising also-rans like Robert Rossen and John Berry. This cycle also has the cachet of being on the "right" (read: Left) side of history. On the premise that it would insult these filmmakers to believe that they did nothing to earn HUAC's opprobrium, Andersen shows that these films evince a critical, leftist perspective.[2]

Rogin's "Kiss Me Deadly: Communism, Motherhood and Cold War Cinema" (1985) is a broader account that includes allegories of atomic anxiety like *Them!* (1954), about gigantic mutant ants overrunning Los Angeles, or nightmarish tales of alien inundation like *Invasion of the Body Snatchers* (1956), in which extraterrestrial pods replace in simulated human forms the citizens of small-town America with conformist ciphers. Only one of the films Rogin considers, *I Was a Communist for the FBI* (1951), represents film rouge. Moreover, Rogin's focus on motherhood casts all his examples as psychodrama, slighting other considerations of politics or genre and suggesting little difference between a *My Son John* and a satirical fantasia like *The Manchurian Candidate* (1962)—a film that splits the difference between anti-Communism, anti-McCarthyism, and spoofs of both, with its flamboyantly demonized mother directly complicit with the Communists in making her brainwashed son into a mindless assassin doing the bidding of the party.

A fuller survey of film rouge clarifies how far *My Son John* stands from the general run. As Rogin notes, the films use conventions of the gangster film, but his claim that they depoliticized the appeals of Communism should be qualified. In nearly every case, these films include a disaffected character who becomes a Communist out of frustration over economic prospects, like the jobless worker of *The Red Menace* (1948); or a political idealist who joins the party because of its progressive promises, like the teacher in *I Was a Communist for the FBI*. In either case, this character becomes disillusioned with Communism in a plot turn meant to expose the falsity of its ideological claims. Yet the connection inevitably points up as well a lurking dissatisfaction with the possibilities of capitalism that did in fact boost the party's roster during the Great Depression, leading many later victims of HUAC, for example, to join. It is to the films' credit that they suggest some of this malaise.

Aside from *My Son John*, no other film in the cycle focuses on the domestic sphere or concerns the "infiltration" of the American family until *Red Nightmare* (1962), an oddity that rang the death knell of the series in the same year that *The Manchurian Candidate*'s hipster sensibility made any entry look square and anachronistic by comparison, and two years before *Dr. Strangelove* drove the final nail into the coffin. In *Red Nightmare*, a father wakes to find his family converted to Communism overnight, a transformation mainly involving robotic behavior in the body-snatchers mold. Even that film moves quickly out of the home into the larger community; indeed, film rouge pays significantly less attention to matters of hearth and home than typical Hollywood fare, another area of overlap with film noir. In *I Was a Communist for the FBI*, two scenes are devoted to establishing the vehement disapproval of the main character's son and brothers over his party membership (his wife is significantly absent), but the bulk of the film concerns his interactions with party functionaries and especially his work in a factory that he runs as a double-agent. In that role, he is in thrall to left-wing unions packed with fellow travelers and ordered by the bosses to favor party members and engineer disabling industrial accidents for anti-Communist workers. Late in the cycle, *The Fearmakers* (1958) concerns a public relations firm that has been taken over, while its patriotic founder was off fighting in the Korean War, by Communists who plot to use it to as a perch from which to manipulate mass opinion and pave the way for a Soviet takeover. Most of the film is set in an office rife with standard-issue Gray Flannel Suit/ Organization Man imagery a la the recent retro-pastiche serial *Mad Men* (which might have derived some of its cheeky visual design from this source). One outlier that does concern a family—*Man on a Tightrope* (1955), directed by HUAC-friendly witness Elia Kazan—depicts them in the context of an unusual workplace, a circus, where they heroically fend off Communist influences.

HUAC's activities had an obviously chilling effect on the American Left and elsewhere over this period, though both HUAC and J. Edgar Hoover as director of the FBI were often at pains (usually brought on by payments of lip service) to distinguish legitimate American liberalism from Communism. Unburdened by such scruples, film rouge seldom hesitates to blur that line or erase it altogether. *I Was a Communist for the FBI* is a veritable anthology of examples, attributing all manner of dissent from the Cold War "consensus" to Communist-front organizations. Detroit's 1943 racial uprisings are ascribed directly to Communist influence, with all civil rights struggles placed under the shadow of doubt. The postwar consolidation of labor unions is imputed to the same fronts that press for women's rights not from any commitment to gender parity, but only to foment social unrest. During a strike, the Communists assault those who cross picket lines with crowbars wrapped in Yiddish newspapers to implicate Jews in the attacks, declaring, "Jews, Catholics—until we get them all fighting, how do we expect to defeat them and establish a Soviet America?" Another party operative whose stated goal is to spread doubt, fear, and demoralization counsels how to turn the HUAC investigations in their favor: "Let them howl their heads off about the rape

of the First Amendment!" Another advises minions to put out
the word that the committee consists of nothing but "fathead
politicians," and then let "the gullible" take it from there. The
film is one of only two in the cycle to depict a HUAC hearing—
the other is the John Wayne vehicle *Big Jim McLain* (1952)—a
proceeding shown as dignified and orderly by contrast to the
anarchy of the Communists, even though if any institution
of the day sought to cast suspicion on progressive causes in
America, it was HUAC. Just as commonly as its conflation of
liberalism and Communism, film rouge equates Communism
with Fascism, typically suggesting that the former is simply a
new mutation of the latter, despite the Soviet alliance with the
United States against Fascism during the Second World War.
The most explicit assertion of this correspondence appears at
the outset of *The Hoaxters* (1952), a documentary produced
by Dore Schary, the head of Metro-Goldwyn Mayer who had
resisted the blacklist longer than any other studio executive,
yet produced this most virulently anti-Communist film of
the series. Vilifying the "masters of deceit"—as the title of
Hoover's feverish 1958 manifesto called Communists—the
film's narrator calls Karl Marx (apparently the King of Russia)
"the fourth pitchman of the apocalypse" in a line of fascist
leaders from Hitler and Mussolini to Hideki Tojo, selling "the
same old snake oil that has brought millions to their knees and
to their graves" with "the only difference that his bottle has a
different label—a red one." A later title reads, "The deadly peril
that faces Democracy today is the deadly parallel that exists
between Communism and similar brands of Totalitarianism ...
namely, Nazism."

Similarly, in *The Fearmakers*, the villains include a physicist
resembling J. Robert Oppenheimer (whose 1954 security
clearance aired the specter of his Communist associations),
a few garden-variety American communists, and a quasi-
fascist or two, all pursuing their nefarious goal of "Peace
at Any Price" as an apparently natural extension of prewar
aspirations to world conquest. The Communists of *The Whip
Hand* (1951), meanwhile, work in harmony alongside former

Nazis in their plot to sap and impurify the American water supply. In reality, of course, though Fascist and Communist states shared authoritarian structures, they occupied opposite ends of the political spectrum. To the extent that film rouge arose to appease HUAC, this strain was especially ironic, since HUAC's previous visit to Hollywood, in 1941, was undertaken to discourage the production of antifascist films like Chaplin's *The Great Dictator* (1940) during the last gasp of American isolationism before the United States entered the war. Expressing a default "official" neutrality, HUAC then declared films such as Chaplin's "prematurely antifascist"—that is, opposing Fascism before the government did. In a majority of cases, blacklisted actors, writers, and directors had been associated with such antifascist activity before, during, or just after the war, including Chaplin, John Garfield, Orson Welles, and dozens of others. In fact, during the 1930s and 1940s, the Communist Popular Front tried to make common cause with non-Communists in the fight against Fascism, drawing in countless artists at all levels of American culture. It was this very activity that typically resulted in the Communist ties that HUAC would later use against them.

The representations of Communism in film rouge are depressingly congruent with the political fantasies spun by HUAC. They propose conspiracies to overthrow American democracy, always presented as nascent and localized but aspiring to global dominion. The ideology of Communism is seldom broached except in the most superficial ways, its partisans depicted as stealth agents passing as normal citizens yet really conspirators, cynical spies, ruthless revolutionaries, self-absorbed operatives, or mere automatons. The danger of these demonic Others impersonating real Americans may register subliminally, but the films tend to place their ultimate faith in the national gut-instinct. Typically, the Communists are generically "foreign," for all that they simulate Americanness. Those of *The Whip Hand*, for example, are characterized as immigrants despite their impeccable Midwestern drawls. *My Son John* is the only example that confronts the emergence of the figure of the Communist from within the American family. In doing so, it raises questions about the dynamics of identity and difference, sameness and otherness, that shoot to the very heart of what Hollywood movies do, and what they are.

One way to describe *My Son John* is as a Leo McCarey movie that suddenly, in its last stretch, turns into an example of film rouge. That characterization, however, understates the intricate manner in which the strains are interwoven in the film. Among what makes it such a suggestive example is the difficulty of disentangling the McCarey "voice" from the impersonal registers that communicate in any film and especially one that functions in part as a kind of time capsule of its era, expressing prevailing attitudes of the day. From an auteurist standpoint, part of the "problem" of *My Son John* is that it is easy to read as McCarey's *most* "personal" film—certainly the one that directly reflects convictions he stated dramatically in public, via his HUAC testimony—yet it is also the *least* immediately congruent with his oeuvre, the least readily amenable to "category e," against-the-grain readings. Film rouge in general resists such analysis, providing essentially univocal statements of reactionary ideology, probably accounting for the lack of critical interest. On the whole, auteurs kept their distance. Jacques Tourneur directed *The Fearmakers*, but he was a relative latecomer to the field whose partisans tried wanly to integrate that film into the filmmaker's canon (as a quasi-sequel to the nominally more respectable *Night of the Demon* [1958], for example) but mainly dismissed it as a minor anomaly. Elia Kazan directed *Man on a Tightrope*, but he was demoted from the promising to the innocuous following his HUAC appearance—though his later film, *A Face in the Crowd*, a reversion to a more critical view of American culture after a series of self-aggrandizing films like *On the Waterfront* (1954) justifying his testimony, did appear on the *Cahiers* ten-best list in 1958. However, Leo McCarey was the only director with claims to something like a full-fledged auteur status to contribute to the cycle.

He was also the only filmmaker to make an anti-Communist film after the war who had made an anti-Nazi film during the war, *Once Upon a Honeymoon*. One of the paradoxes of the time was that antifascist commitments of the 1930s and early 1940s translated into pro-Communist suspicions in the late 1940s and 1950s. Indeed, the screenwriter of *Once Upon a Honeymoon,* Sheridan Gibney, was an avowed leftist who was ostracized in the second wave of the blacklist. McCarey, meanwhile, was a charter member beginning in 1944 of the Motion Picture Alliance, a group dedicated to the "preservation of American ideals" that stood against Communism even during the U.S.-Soviet alliance in the war and supplied the first cooperative witnesses to HUAC. This membership may have placed him above suspicion for HUAC, but the presence of *Once Upon a Honeymoon* in his filmography still complicates any reading of *My Son John* and McCarey's relation to HUAC.

Moreover, evidence suggests McCarey's efforts to temper the anti-Communism of *My Son John*. As it happens, the credit for screenwriting went to arbitration with the Writers' Guild, a process becoming increasingly common as Hollywood production models became less centralized through the 1950s. Submitted as evidence were McCarey's original story, "Mother Story," drafts of an original script by John Lee Mahin, drafts of a subsequent rewrite by McCarey in collaboration with Myles Connolly, a "final white script" (a transcript of the film's final cut), and a separately filed monologue of John's final address titled "Commencement Speech" and credited solely to McCarey. Only three months before the film's release, the guild granted story credit and primary screenwriting credit to McCarey, with Connolly cited as cowriter and the consolation prize of "adaptation" credit granted to Mahin, apparently on the premise that he had "adapted" McCarey's story, even though he had written himself a very different earlier treatment. A review of these materials provides extensive insight into the genesis of the project. McCarey's hiring of both Mahin and Connolly suggests an attempt to achieve some kind of ideological balance, since Mahin was well known as a conservative and anti-Communist, while Connolly had a reputation as a moderate Catholic. His most recent credit was the screenplay for Frank Capra's *State of the Union* (1948), a fictive exposé of corruption in the Republican Party that was easily readable as a not-so-veiled rebuke to HUAC. Earlier, Connolly had contributed uncredited rewrites to Capra's *Mr. Smith Goes to Washington* (1939), targeted by HUAC in its earlier incarnation as prematurely antifascist much as Capra's later films were deemed suspect in the McCarthy era.

Mahin's original script follows his own treatment and differs substantially from the script McCarey shot. Mahin's version is much closer to the standard conventions of film rouge, with a lurid, melodramatic streak throughout rather than the bold turn that McCarey's film ultimately veers into. In the original script, the Jeffersons are a working-class family, the father a factory worker whose coarseness is signified by a succession of "ain't"'s and dropped g's in his unlettered speech. This blue-collar background makes John's conversion into a highbrow intellectual and crypto-Communist seem more extreme. McCarey's version makes the father a schoolteacher, and though something of the anti-intellectual strain remains, he is as much a part of the postwar information-and-service economy as John himself. In the Mahin script John is drawn much less ambiguously, rendering him more effete and less sympathetic from the start. His traitorous activity is specified—he has passed classified papers to Soviet agents—and in his last scene, he admits his collusion directly to his mother, as he never does in the film, devolving thereafter into the menacing malefactor of McCarthyite lore. Mahin's treatment suggests that Lucy "lets it look as if she is insane" rather than to "further expose her son."[3] Despite this tantalizing possibility, she is treated in the script as a much more fully fledged hysteric than the Lucille of McCarey's film, so much so that she goes so far as to shoot her son to prevent him from pursuing his nefarious plot. The rest of the script unfolds in a courtroom during her trial for attempted murder—TRIGGER MOTHER TRIAL! shrieks an imagined headline—the emotional thermostat set so high that

John finally breaks down and confesses publicly to treason to save her.

McCarey collaborated with Connolly on an extensive rewrite subsequently. The finished film hews almost exactly to this script, which retains fragments of Mahin's but reorients the material entirely, opening the dim and complicated portal between standard-issue McCarthyite propaganda and the more variegated world of Leo McCarey. The family dynamics are brought firmly into the foreground, displacing most of the intrigue and locating paranoia in the family structure itself so intently that this becomes the essential subject of the film. The McCarey/Connolly script tamps down the overt hostility between father and son, which plays in the Mahin version as unbridled hatred. In Mahin it is the father, not Lucille, who makes John swear on the Bible in a cascade of Oedipal loathing, whereupon John taunts him openly: "I didn't realize you were that stupid, because if I was [a Communist], that revered publication wouldn't mean a thing to me."[4] In the film, Dan is initially reassured by John's oath but realizes himself that an atheist would not be bound by it, a caveat John dismisses with his usual weary impatience. Though John dramatically outs himself as a Communist spy in his last speech in the film, the nature of his malfeasance remains otherwise obscure beyond garden-variety party membership and the mysterious collusion with Ruth Carlin.

Overall, the McCarey/Connolly script greatly reduces the range of the action and the extent of interactions among multiple characters. Mahin sets scenes in the legion hall, outside a movie theater, in a neighborhood bar, at a maiden aunt's boarding house, and other locations, including action involving Ruth Carlin. Production records indicate that some of these scenes were shot, as expenses are listed over several weeks for the boarding house location in the film's shooting ledger. According to the same source, an actress was also paid to play Carlin, and her casting was announced even after the production had wrapped—Irene Watson, later to appear in a role nearly as invisible, as Mrs. Thorwald, the murdered wife in *Rear Window* (1954). Not only does none of this material appear in the final cut, however, it does not appear in the shooting script, suggesting that McCarey filmed some impromptu amalgam of the two scripts with an eye to the editing room.

Even material from the McCarey/Connolly script is excised from the finished film. The opening scene of the script, for example, depicts Dan at the "Little Red Schoolhouse" leading his students in the "Pledge of Allegiance."[5] Including this scene would have established Dan as a figure of benevolent authority; deleting it lays the groundwork for the bombastic, ineffectual bumbler the film introduces us to. McCarey's minimalist tendencies surface distinctly in this streamlining. As a result, the action of the film takes place almost entirely around the Jefferson house. Brief excursions to the church as well as the street scene of Dan's auto accident are handled in a terse, clipped manner, giving little sense of the larger surround. They do not have the effect of opening up the film spatially to any significant degree. The scenes in Washington DC involve claustrophobic interiors (John's office, Ruth Carlin's apartment), delimited exteriors viewed through the FBI surveillance cameras tracking Lucille, disorienting patched-together location shots, or defamiliarizing back-projections, as in the tense riverside meeting between Stedman and Lucille. All these examples lend an increasingly dream-like element to these sequences, a quality that bleeds into the final scenes in the Jefferson house as the film lumbers to its deranged climax.

The restriction of so much of the action to the house gives the film something of the feeling of a chamber-play, anxiously enclosed upon itself. Despite occasional noirish shadings of light, McCarey largely eschews the Gothic treatment of space that directors of melodrama like Hitchcock, Lang, Minnelli, Ophuls, or other auteurs crafted. The spider-web shadows of Hitchcock's *Suspicion* (1941), the imposing walls that seem to close in on the characters in Lang's *House by the River* (1948) or *Secret Beyond the Door* (1948), the stairway banisters that become entrapping prison bars in Ophuls's *The Reckless*

Moment (1949), or the unsettling clash of garish colors with subdued hues in the institutional spaces of Minnelli's *The Cobweb* (1955) all exemplify these directors' penchant for enlivening space, conferring visual energy and motion upon the inanimate matter of static interiors. Such expressionist designs are alien to McCarey, whose typical mise-en-scène is studiedly *in*expressive, lacking the intricate detail of Minnelli's décors or the lush textures of Ophuls's interiors. In McCarey, inert matter tends to stay inert, and to express, if anything, that very state, at best becoming an obstacle—a car that won't go, a table to fall over—and attesting to the failure of insensate matter to cooperate in the realm of human intention. The clearest departure from the pattern, the grandmother's idyllic hermitage in *Love Affair* and *Affair to Remember*, where everything seems to vibrate with inspired vitality, is a lovely exception that proves the general rule.

Against these inscrutable backdrops the situational interactions of McCarey's characters come into sharp relief, more harshly than usual in *My Son John*. In the thrillers of Hitchcock or the melodramas of Douglas Sirk, subtexts are siphoned off into the mise-en-scène, visualizing characters' inner states—the disquieting flashes of red in Hitchcock's *Marnie* or the sickly green lights playing over characters' faces in *All That Heaven Allows* (1955). In McCarey, though subtexts proliferate, no such outlets present themselves, giving the sense that the feelings have nowhere to go; in this curiously deadened visual landscape, the emotional climate of the film takes on a stalled, rankling quality. Never has the sense of hovering anticipation that lingers even over McCarey's comedies been more ubiquitous than it is in *My Son John*, all the more pungently so because one never quite knows what anyone is waiting for. It is further amplified by a decisive turn in the structure. Where Mahin's script most often features mother, father, and son together, McCarey—with his preference for duos over any other collocation—resolutely divides the characters into pairs engaged in rotating, successive colloquies, as in a joyless roundelay or a Chekhov play: Lucille and Dan,

John and Lucille, Lucille and John, John and Dan, Dan and Lucille, Lucille and Stedman, and so on. This resolve brings with it a narrative awkwardness familiar in McCarey's work, as characters report to one another what we have already seen dramatized. It also imparts a tensed, fugue-like atmosphere, as if the film were holding its breath.

Performance and gesture as text

One effect of the stark interiors is to offset details of performance. As often in McCarey's work these are intricate, especially in the cases of Lucille and John, and in contrast with the vacated, nearly abstract backdrops. As Lucille, Helen Hayes combines precision of speech—in the tempo and modulation of line deliveries and in the quality of intonation, nuanced yet exact—with a looser, unpredictable disposition of the body. In this she joins a lineage of ideal McCarey performers, from Groucho Marx to Cary Grant, Irene Dunne, Bing Crosby, and—surprisingly enough—Ingrid Bergman, all of whom communicate in their performances for McCarey as much through gesture and facial expression as through dialogue, often in counterpoint to the films' verbal texts. Groucho Marx's delivery is so fleet and flat that it is sometimes only his insouciant slouch, suggestive wriggle of the eyebrows, and ribald flick of a cigar that make his sarcastic meaning belatedly apparent. Grant's and Crosby's sidelong glances and wry double-takes provide unexpected commonalities between these otherwise quite different actors; Grant plays them up in his manner of positioning himself sideward to the action, angling his head stiffly and striking brief serial poses, almost Kabuki-like, as a witty, unspoken comment on the goings-on around him, while the more relaxed Crosby merely purses his lips or conveys the slightest edge of surprise with the slightest widening of the eyes. Dunne's controlled yet fluttery movements of the hands and slightly dazed, quizzical looks, lips parted in a constant, dreamy half-smile, were never more charmingly showcased than in *The Awful Truth* and *Love*

Affair. What makes Bergman surprising in this lineup is her adoption of a professional Hollywood smoothness with her ethereal bearing, both of which McCarey exploits and subverts in *The Bells of St. Mary's*—as witness the scene where she teaches a boy to box and dances madly to illustrate footwork, her frock tails flying, then, after being knocked silly by an unlucky punch, works her jaw back and forth like an old slapstick pro. The combination in this performance of physicality and earthiness with spiritual intensity anticipates Bergman's later work with Roberto Rossellini in a way that none of her other Hollywood work did.

Advance publicity for *My Son John* heralded Helen Hayes's return to the screen after decades forging a legendary reputation on stage as the "First Lady of the American Theater." The groundwork for that reputation was already laid when she appeared in several films in the early 1930s as sound came in. Despite her theatrical training, she was supposed to help bring a "naturalistic" performance style to movies after the presumably more exaggerated, gesture-based, quasi-pantomime of the silent years. As Catherine in the first film version of Hemingway's *A Farewell to Arms* (1932), Hayes gives a movingly natural performance delineated to a degree unusual for the era by gesture, especially by contrast to her rigid and taciturn costar, Gary Cooper. She has a way of clasping one arm with the hand of the other, for example, that manages to convey her character's confidence and agitation at once, prefiguring her work in *My Son John*. Her Academy Award-winning performance in *The Sin of Madelon Claudet* (1930) is more histrionic, more like the other film work of her stage contemporaries, such as Jeanne Eagels's stunningly intense, hyper-fidgety characterization in *The Letter* (1929), and Hayes's uses of gesture in that film are correspondingly larger, even overwrought. In *My Son John*, her "return" performance strikes a remarkable balance, at once harking back to early styles of film acting in its gestural dimensions— much like Lillian Gish in her "comeback" roles of the 1950s, especially *The Night of the Hunter*—and dovetailing in its interiority with trends of Method acting emerging in postwar cinema at the time.

Especially in recent years, the concept of gesture has emerged as an important category for film theory, because it constitutes a nonverbal means of communication with a language of its own, like the visual structures of cinema itself, providing a bridge between film actors' performances and film form. Even classical film theory had reason to deal with the status of the gesture. For the Soviet proponents of montage, it was largely a holdover from theater that threatened the primacy of editing by claiming meanings of its own in performance rather than yielding to the conjunctive logics of montage. Eisenstein reconfigured gesture as a figure of montage, referring to "the movement of the dynamic gesture within the frame, and the static gesture dividing the frame graphically."[6] As an opponent of montage, Bazin embraced the gesture as profoundly cinematic for much the same reasons, particularly in his writings on Chaplin.[7] Always a factor in theories of performance, oratory, and rhetoric, ideas about gesture have figured centrally in efforts to theorize film acting, especially in the wake of poststructuralism, and at a nexus between performance and cinematic form. In a similar spirit, Giorgio Agamben writes of a gestural cinema in which performers' gestures at once correspond to the "gestures" of enunciation (cutting, framing, and so on) and articulate a parallel language so intricate that it multiplies units of meaning and so deconstructs the unity of the film image which Bazin had celebrated.[8] Recent work on "figural" cinema by Nicole Brenez, Adrian Martin, D. N. Rodowick, and others proceeds along similar lines, with films' meanings understood as divided between being representational in the art-historical sense (i.e., not abstract) and metaphorical in the rhetorical sense (i.e., figurative language). Much of this work is dedicated to defining a so-called "cinema of the body," with the cinematic body understood as a "figure" in just this divided sense, as a material presence and a semiotic emblem at once, and with the gesture providing a sort of bridge between these facets, simultaneously bodily expression and visual signification.

The 1950s auteurists anticipated these theoretical implications and influenced many of them. For them, the gesture bears inspiriting traces of silent cinema, preserving the spontaneity that is supposed to coexist with the self-reflexive and the mechanized in auteur cinema. It also constitutes an integral feature of mise-en-scène and describes an element that alternately characterizes an auteur's signature, like the gestures in films by Preminger or Ray, or eludes it in potentially salutary ways. Noames's treatment of McCarey in *Cahiers* implies a strong gestural dimension in casting McCarey's figures as tantamount to "beasts," bereft of ordinary articulations and thrown back upon gestural expression.

In McCarey's films, gestures define performance in basic ways, expressing forms of freedom associated with the domain of play and creative activity that his films typically celebrate. The myriad performances and plays-within-the-film that recur throughout his work often link speech to laboriousness and gesture to a beguiling escape from language, defining an effortless space within a world otherwise made up of obstacles, of which language is one. The tedious fairy tales Sam tells his daughter in *Good Sam* contrast with the physical comedy he acts out alongside the stories, just as in *The Bells of St. Mary's* the stilted "lines" the students recite by rote in their Christmas pageant are at odds with the inspired bits of stage business they make up as they go along. One might say, in fact, that this gestural level of performance is the very location of McCarey's vaunted principle of improvisation. Hayes's performance in *My Son John* is emblematic for many reasons. No performance in McCarey's oeuvre is rooted more deeply in the gestural—and this is the only McCarey film (except *Satan Never Sleeps*) that suggests few possibilities of entry into that domain of free play and creativity that his other films yearn for. (Even *Make Way for Tomorrow* provides the exhilarating Manhattan interlude before the final parting.) In this film, Hayes's performance becomes the text through which the film plays out many of its most potent, confused, and eloquent contradictions.

By the time we first see Lucille, we already know she is a problem. She keeps the family waiting for reasons they cannot conceive. When she first appears on the porch, her stance is humorously adversarial and apologetic, self-effacing, at the same time. This is an attitude that defines the family's interactions. One of the football-playing sons has just tried to usurp the driver's seat on the grounds that Dan seems "nervous"—the descriptor the parents will compulsively apply to John and to each other—and the father protests jokingly with an odd, overexplicit yet clipped intonation on "ner-vuss," much like the fussy pronunciation he gives to "waay-TING." The other son (or the same one, since they are interchangeable) ribs Lucille by calling her "Sweater Girl," a gibe that would seem undeniably eroticized in nearly any other context. Does he mean to imply that he thinks she has been upstairs fantasizing about movie stars, daydreaming of Lana Turner? Nothing we see justifies any such implication. The joke strikes one of the off-notes that make up these scenes, but Lucille tartly welcomes the faux flirtation, holding her own in the teasing skirmishes and "flirting," in her turn, with just about every man in the movie except her husband.

This is not, to be sure, the scorching private bickering already disclosed as a routine feature of American family life in movies like, say, *The Magnificent Ambersons* (1942), apt to turn vicious on a dime, and to wound. In *My Son John*, it is apparently taken by its participants to indicate affections of a sort. Do they take it as a symptom of domestic health, preferable to genteel repressions? In any case, despite the obvious heedlessness of her husband and sons, the film does not make it difficult to imagine that Lucille might well wish to defer her entry into the familial fray.

She waves both hands dramatically to goad the men into the car, bobbing her head in time with the undulations of her own arms, a broad, unwieldy gesture that is the first of the series. The motion is comic in its silent-movie exaggeration, part of the fabric of teasing yet dismissive, like shooing a cat. As the film develops, these gestures draw increasing attention to themselves, though attracting little notice from other characters, who try to ignore them. They define Lucille's character and the spectator's relation to her. Virtually Brechtian, they have something of a distancing effect, at times playing as stylized tics that undermine the naturalism of Hayes's performance due to their excess. Undeniably, they connote spontaneity of a sort, seeming at times involuntary and suggesting a discomfiting loss of control. The arc of the performance ends with Lucille's "nervous breakdown," and its burden is to encompass such an extreme, enacting it plausibly through the medium of a character otherwise presented as feisty, independent, possessed of an unusual inner strength. A dialectic of intense identification and estrangement surrounds the character, as it does the whole film, and Lucille's gestures are a large part of what sets that dialectic in play, asserting her tenuous authority, revealing her vulnerability and ambivalence, and ultimately expressing her profound sense of otherness.

In the scene of the last supper before her sons' departure for battle, Lucille shrugs off an offer of wine a bit too urgently, hoists a glass to salute her absent son too robustly, and snaps her fingers too sharply in reply to yet another teasing sally that might well play as affectionate if they were not all starting to seem so relentless, so dire. Perhaps these gestures are meant to signify something appealing, a dynamic vitality, but they always seem a bit too much, out of synch with the ordinary rhythms of the conversations around her. But who *wouldn't* want to be out of synch with those? We can easily see that Lucille dotes on her husband and sons, yet her own participation in all the good-natured joshing indicates some awareness of herself as a principle of emotional surplus. Most often her gesticulations pick up where her voice leaves off. Just as the blank aspect of McCarey's mise-en-scène leaves feeling hovering, anxiously unexpressed, Lucille's gestures point to the unspoken words of one unaccustomed to being heard. All that teasing, it seems, leaves something still repressed after all.

This procession of seemingly benign men—her husband and sons, the priest, the doctors, the FBI agent—forms a galumphing little march of concern for Lucille. It is the very McCareyian moderation of variety in the scenes' tempos and textures that prompts us to suspect that there might be something wrong with all these solicitous attentions. The joyless undertone of the teasing becomes more distinct. Do *they* suspect that what she was doing in keeping them waiting was composing herself, erasing her sadness, hiding the signs of her grief? Despite the emotional detachment implied in their jokes, they maintain a recognizable familial protocol of patrolling one another for signs of whatever is unexpressed, not in any apparent hope that it will be, but in the evident expectation that it must not be. Like the heroine of a Gothic paranoid fiction—say, the one in Charlotte Perkins Gilman's *The Yellow Wallpaper* (1892)—Lucille really *is* the object of a conspiracy, one that is, within its own suffocating terms, bent on ensuring her well-being. Glances are repeatedly exchanged around her on the tacit theory that she will not notice; her gestures are our clearest indication that she does.

The strangest of these gestures occurs in the film's first third, in the scene when the birdlike doctor descends bearing his pills for Lucille. Out of nowhere, Lucille thrusts her arm outward in a sudden swoop, clasps her fist in mid-air, holds the pose for a second, slightly bent over, then slowly uncurls her fingers, leaning forward to scan her open palm and, finding it empty, tilting her face upward, gazing at her husband, grimacing bizarrely, and unleashing a guttural, breathy quasi-laugh. Viewers of McCarey's films may be unsurprised at other characters' lack of reaction to this display, but the pointed nonresponse is more disquieting than usual in the context of what had seemed to be shaping up as an exercise in domestic realism.

Even if we attribute some literal motive—an attempt to catch a fly?—Lucille's spasmodic motion remains unreadable unless we begin to consider these gestures as expressions of a certain agency by other means. Hayes's performance depends on a quick shuttling between indications of a latent pathology and a heightened cogency and confidence, custodian of the family's emotional and moral life. In this scene, the turn is especially striking, as Lucille's staunch verbal refusal of the pills is dismissed but the gesture at least succeeds in halting the action for a moment. Lucille's lone power, it seems, resides in such deferral—keeping them waiting, throwing them off a bit, slowing for an instant the progress of their logics.

Her son John, too, even more elaborately, is defined as a problem before he is introduced, far from the only thing the two have in common as characters. Prior to his appearance, the film marks his absence with an uncharacteristically emphatic shot of his empty chair. It is not just this lack the shot denotes but a structural separation: the chair occupies a space of its own, alone on its own side of the long dining table. Had he been present, the sense of John's being placed apart would have been still more unmistakable. Though no explicit disapproval is vented about his absence, Lucille feels compelled all the same to stand up for him, to justify his failure to appear at the going-away rite. When she says that John has sent his love by phone, Dan does air mild doubts on the matter. Like Lucille, John keeps them waiting and occupies the wrong emotional position in relation to the rest, but while Lucille loves the family too much, apparently, John loves it too little.

As soon as he arrives, it is clear that he perceives exactly the troubling dynamics the film has been gently exposing. It is for this reason that his presence instantly charges the atmosphere with a current of subliminal menace, fulfilling the portent of his portrayal under the opening credits as a dark, featureless silhouette, the shadowy villain he does eventually become, after a fashion. Before his ultimate demonization as a stand-in for the Red Menace, however, the unspoken threat he represents is much closer to home. It is that he could at any moment pull away the insulating drape in which the family has so comfortably shrouded itself.

John's manner conveys an underlying weariness that shows he is, indeed, all too well acquainted with the ways of this family. Toward his father, he cultivates a stance of guarded neutrality, toward his mother a kind of genial, detached warmth. In the McCareyian mode, he is struck anew by her spontaneity when, on his appearance, she reveals some of the emotions she has been restraining, and he is both troubled and moved. He intervenes when Dan cuts Lucille off, curtly interrupting his father in turn to allow his mother to speak. If there were any possibility in the film of the kind of direct emotional connections McCarey's movies aspire toward, it would be between Lucille and John. What gives the film its elegiac edge is how visible the traces of that connection are; the film *does* follow the McCareyian process by which each comes to perceive the other anew, but it cannot conceive any way to sanction that outcome, lurching sadly into shrill melodrama as an effect of that incapacity.

John's attitudes toward the family connote a long familiarity converted by force of will into a studied indifference capable of encompassing residual affections but always slightly chilled by exasperation. He recognizes the policing functions of the family and has clearly devised an arsenal of strategies for neutralizing it. "John, you look worried," Lucille remarks, scanning his face, though the blunt accompanying shot shows that he looks no different from usual; to this he replies crisply, "Now let's not go into how I look again," and Lucille quietly withdraws. These are the rhythms of the film from the moment John appears, gaining tension alongside the usual McCareyian lurch-and-lag: hesitant advance, tentative parry, meek retreat—not unlike the equally excruciating cadences of another roughly contemporary study in paralytic domestic dysfunction in America, Eugene O'Neil's *Long Day's Journey into Night* (written in 1941–42 but first published in 1956).

Identity and difference on the horizon of sameness

John's entry rearranges the molecules of the film's energies to such an extent that it admits a passing instance of expressive mise-en-scène at the moment of his appearance. The mirror that hangs in the Jefferson foyer, formerly one of the obdurate things that make up the décor as a whole, suddenly becomes a harbinger of meaning. Signifying mirrors are staples of auteurist cinema and analysis, usually as markers of a previously occulted self-reflection manifesting itself. For example, Douglas Sirk tends to use mirrors to assert a strong divide between his films' self-consciousness and their characters' obliviousness. In *Imitation of Life* (1959), Sirk cuts repeatedly to reflections in mirrors of the film's chief dolt, Lora (Lana Turner), just after she has dispensed one of her pert or self-dramatizing idiocies. In these instances, she is doubled in the image, suggesting the split between her self-image as a benign figure and the actuality of her destructive cluelessness. Yet, while the viewer may (or may not) note the doubling gesture, she herself remains blithely unaware. The mirror reflections in *Love Affair* suggest a precedent in McCarey's work, and they too indicate a lack of self-awareness on characters' parts, though mirrors in the visual arts typically connote extreme self-consciousness—see, for example, Parmigianino's great painting *Self-Portrait in a Convex Mirror* (c. 1524) and John Ashbery's poetic gloss on it in 1975—or, at the opposite extreme, narcissism. In *Love Affair*, neither Terry nor Michel appears in reflection; each is gazing at the object itself, not its reflection, which only we see and of which they are unaware. In Michel's case, the treatment is doubly suggestive, as the script calls for Michel to look into the mirror at the moment when he sees his painting;[9] in McCarey's realization, he is positioned with his back to the mirror, looking at the off-screen painting which only the viewer sees reflected. While in Sirk the mirror imagery provides a trenchant critique, in McCarey, as so often in his work, the lack of self-consciousness is a *positive* value. It is what enables the epiphanic experience of the characters in these scenes; the point is that rather than being mired in disabling self-reflection, they are in direct contact with the object of their own gaze, and with reality itself.

In *My Son John*, the figure depends on an uncharacteristically intricate mix of staging, performance, and camera placement. In a medium long shot scaled exactly to encompass the oblique action, John extricates himself from Lucille's embrace as Dan edges uneasily around them into the right of the frame. Peripherally, John notices the shuffling motion reflected in the mirror and turns to the left; we see an expression of distaste flicker across his face as he recognizes the image of his father reflected there, but John mutes this expression as he turns back to Dan, extending a stiff hand in greeting. In one sense, this figure performs a narrative function, continuing the pattern of indirection in the family dynamics. It is one of McCarey's trademark "small moments," which usually gain resonance from their unemphatic, passing character—the opposite number of the "too-long" intervals. The unusual stress here demands our attention to this "byplay" (as McCarey himself referred to moments like this in scripts and notes). That John sees his father's reflection before he sees his father himself is pointedly established as a distinction of note. Obviously, it sets up the Oedipal dimension in a mode of projection. We can assume from the context of McCarey's career that what he would likely "want" for the characters is that they see one another as they "really are." The mirror play suggests in passing the obstructed state of this desired condition.

The line of dialogue immediately preceding this moment is telling. Lucille throws the door open and the film catches its slow breath in an instant of stilled perception as she takes him in on the threshold, the cherished object finally embodied, genuinely present. As John surrenders to her awkward embrace, she intones one of her frequent unfinished sentences: "You *are* –!" Like those of most of McCarey's many hesitant speakers—such as Terry/Irene Dunne, whose lines in the script for *Love Affair* are a farrago of broken phrases, undone thoughts, and stuttering dashes—the line appears just like this in the McCarey script, exactly as Hayes delivers it. In the film its incompletion gets somewhat lost in the shuffle. Probably if Lucille finished her thought it would equate to something like, "You are really here!" or "It *is* you!" But the line—"You *are* –"—gains resonance in retrospect as the film's main question gradually unfurls: What *is* he? Unachieved, fragmentary phrasings pose the question in different forms, sometimes relating to how John "looks" (worried, nervous) or whether or not he *is* "one": "I never said you *were* one," Dan capitulates. "I just said you *sounded* like … " Finally, in a moment of surprising poise and good-humored equanimity, John takes matters in hand and evenly pledges on the Bible the exact phrase demanded, but so rarely heard, by the House Un-American Activities Committee: "I am not now nor have I ever been a member of the Communist party."

The word "Communist" has been spoken before this point only once previously in the film, in a soft-pedaled form. Dan's preferred term is "scummies," while others choose to stay mum. John is the first to apply the word to himself, albeit in a mode of negation. His denial is both strangely casual and shocking, a direct reference in a jaunty tone to what has been so elaborately evaded until this point. It further reflects the quality of knowingness that defines his character, a matter-of-fact cut-to-the-chase that implicitly rebukes his parents' dithering, half-articulated speculations and simpering, shrinking insinuations. In the McCarey play of knowing and unknowing, he "knows" they "know." From the start, they know that he is, he *is* … something, something *other*—but *what*? In a genuinely dogmatic tract there would be but one alternative. In *My Son John*, the hidden referent floats and bobs in shifting currents of doubt. Robert Warshow postulates this genteel hypothesis: "[T]hough nothing is said of this, one feels that he might be a homosexual."[10] James Baldwin is less polite: John is "acting out all of his mother's terrors, including and especially the role of flaming faggot, which is his father's terror, too."[11]

As John, Robert Walker brings levels of meaning to the role comparable to those of a later portrayal of another errant son, Anthony Perkins in *Psycho* (1960). Like Perkins, Walker was known for playing sensitive, even neurotic boy-next-door-types—in films like *Since You Went Away* (1944) or *The Clock*

(1945) for Walker, *The Friendly Persuasion* (1956) and *Fear Strikes Out* (1957) for Perkins—a bit too fey and winsome to qualify as "all-American," perhaps, but boyishly likeable and sympathetic all the same. As he would with Perkins, Alfred Hitchcock cast Walker brilliantly against type, as the psychotic, murderous, Oedipally fixated crypto-queer Bruno in *Strangers on a Train* (1951). That the same timid young man who had wooed Jennifer Jones and Judy Garland was now stalking Farley Granger and strangling bespectacled women in cold blood gave the film an added kick, to put it mildly, and McCarey's casting of Walker in *My Son John* taps quite directly into that performance in more ways than one. For Baldwin, Walker's portrayal of John is a "gleefully vicious parody of the wayward son" that "does a great deal to demystify" the film's homiletics. Walker, he goes on, "plays it for all it's worth, absolutely heartless and hilarious."[12] To say that Warshow, from his nominally liberal anti-Communist perspective, perceives none of the comic overtones of Walker's characterization or the film's treatment overall is an understatement. Warshow can see only the character's intellectual and spiritual rigidity.

Yet these comic elements are crucial, darkened as they are by the echoes of Walker's Hitchcockian turn. Indeed, Walker recycles a number of the distinctive tropes from his performance as Bruno, including his sideward manner of communicating derision, especially for fatherly authority, with a discreet downward tilt of the chin and upward roll of the eyes, or a stifled but sibilant sigh. When he congratulates the priest on his sermon, he draws himself up into a hunch-shouldered simulation of awe and fans his hands out in a parody of fawning praise. Few would be able to miss the coruscating irony or—given its sly, aslant delivery—know how to counter it. Like Bruno's, John's disdain surfaces rarely, but once it does it might always be lurking, seething under the surface. That is how his mother reads him, clearly, and we are given many vantage points from which to share her perspective. Yet the character's placement in general and the comic shadings in particular complicate that perspective; they attest that John's derision is shared at least in part by the overarching consciousness guiding the film.

An unlikely but telling precedent of Walker's performance in McCarey's filmography is Charles Laughton's in *Ruggles of Red Gap*. The key to the humor in that case is the clash between the horror Ruggles feels at the vulgarities of the hayseed family he has been consigned to serve and his professional obligation to conceal that reaction. This distaste, however restrained, must also be communicated to the audience, drawing the spectator into a conspiratorial participation in Ruggles's aversion. Laughton adopts a flamboyant stiffness, a variant of the McCareyian comic nonresponse, with a rigidity in keeping with a butler's formality but sufficiently stylized to convey the underlying mortification. Walker's performance draws on similar resources but has the added burden of having to exhibit the strangulated nature of the humor, a quality that defines it, making it hard for a viewer to discern an appropriate response.

Common as it is in McCarey's films, this comedy of excruciation has never been taken further in his work, the discomfort it elicits never more pungently asserted. In this regard, the auteur-meter registers in an especially high range, since this comedy might be altogether invisible to a viewer unfamiliar with McCarey's career—and might also, after all, be discounted as nothing but the fanciful projection of the starry-eyed auteurist in the first place. The scene often cited as the film's most embarrassing, when Dan conks John with the Bible, has never been earmarked by any critic as funny at all, never mind deliberately so. But to a student of McCarey, the Laurel-and-Hardy reverb of the scene is unmistakable—in its suddenness, in the disconnect between the extent of Dan's Hardy-like pique and the meagerness of his onset (a slightness punctuated by the comic-strip sound effect that accompanies the bop on the head), the little pause on the benumbed aftermath and the frozen double-takes of the stunned combatants, the mismatched cutting that renders John's subsequent tumble over the table as pure surreal slapstick.

If this comedy can be called "hilarious," qua Baldwin, it is a stifled hilarity of a kind McCarey has explored often. In many of his films, it finds an outlet in terminal bouts of uncontrollable laughter shared by lovers, outbursts that stand as the ultimate expression of their true bonds. In the last line of *Love Affair*, Terry insults Michel inadvertently—"If you can paint, then I can walk … *Anything* can happen!"—but instead of taking umbrage he joins with Terry in a joint recognition of the unintended implication, and they dissolve into the helpless laughter that ends the film. Despite Lu's exasperation with her husband in *Good Sam*, she too cannot refrain from laughing at his antics, and once again the film ends in a duet of uncontrollable laughter expressing the profound mutuality of the characters' enjoyment of each other. Similar examples clutter McCarey's oeuvre, including *My Son John*, where shared laughter also functions as code. In this case, however, it suggests alienation rather than connectedness, exclusion rather than inclusion. The ostensibly easygoing chaffing that defines the family's congress is another of the rites that John understands implicitly, but his own teasing provokes unease. For example, his joke that his father's legion hall should send out for more beer is greeted with a perturbed silence—like McCarey's proverbial fart at the dinner table—before Dan and Lucille affect forced laughter that John awkwardly joins in. The same dynamic in reverse, with John feigning a sickly gale of laughter that his parents feebly join, plays out after Dan's corny joke about the Communist Party having reported the results of next year's elections. In these examples, we see how John's repeated efforts to cooperate in the family rituals serve only to set him further apart. Even before any intimations arise of his Communist allegiances, it is clear that John's segregation from his family is both elected and imposed. For his parents, his difference from them is his salient trait; constantly on the alert, they see the signs of it everywhere. John's affect of brisk resignation shows that none of this is new to him. His demeanor is indeed that of the closeted son, confident in his own integrity despite the expedient indignity of having to keep his secret from people to whom it is unexplainable, who would be able to understand it only in their own terms, yet to whom he remains, in some mysterious way, deeply connected. John's participation in the family's customs are always a bit off-stride because, well known as they are to him, he views them from without, from a distance—a position not unlike the one the spectator has gradually been ushered into. The family's pettiness, its complacency, its thoughtless clamor, its marginalization of Lucille—these are the features we have been prodded to note even before John appears, and they are the ones that are amplified in our view under his keen, resentful scrutiny.

To suggest that *My Son John* produces images of difference unusual in a Hollywood movie may seem counterintuitive, given that the homogeneity of its cast and the didacticism of its "message" place it, in a way, quite squarely into the middle of Cold War cinema. Indeed, especially in its classical phase, Hollywood functioned as a virtual sameness-machine, motored by normative identifications. In many accounts, cinematic identification is itself a homogenizing dynamic, those with the privilege to "identify" desiring images of themselves. But the production of sameness has always required the production of difference, which is why it is equally possible to argue, as many theorists have, that the film apparatus is geared to othering and demonization. Difference must be evoked in order to be effaced, however committed a cultural institution like the studio system may have been to disbar it. So delimited is the range of identities represented in Classical Hollywood cinema that even the most demonized can come to resemble the "same" on that narrow horizon. In other words, the institution's drive to reproduce sameness produces difference in such proximity that its appearance threatens to collapse the distinction and undo the whole operation. Certainly, this dynamic is common at the level of sexual difference—the one the institution could rarely find a way to exclude entirely—but a universalizing impulse in the typology of persons across the board starts to seem like a dialectic in disguise, as sameness and difference unexpectedly trade places. Complicit as it may be in spectators' narcissistic projections, cinematic identification can also be the vehicle by which this dialectic becomes visible, as fluid, unpredictable, and uncontrollable as identification is in process. What makes *My Son John* unusual is precisely the identificatory access it opens to characters who function in the film as principles of difference, while barring access to the one character, that of the father, who most seems to speak for the film's "message."

It is not surprising to observe the congruity in *My Son John* of the figures of the homosexual and the Communist, since their conflation was a common homophobic trope of the Cold War era. Baldwin's response, however, attests that the film provides ample space for queer identifications with John. Even if we grant that the film detours into a strategic demonization of the character, he remains available for much of the film as a site of engagement. Lucille's intense if troubled emotional investment in him signals the spectator in turn, as a crucial spur to our own identifications. Indeed, for much of the film, our allegiances align along a complicated axis with both John and Lucille, who are figured as counterparts of difference within the family structure. Lucille harps on their former intimacy and abiding affinity. When she "pleaded" for his education, she tells him, "they teased me that you were my favorite"—a line recalling Lucy's colloquy with George in *Make Way for Tomorrow*. "I know every line, ever curve of that face," Lucille says, expressing an intimacy so raw that John can only ignore it. It is a rawness we may remember in one of their last scenes together, when she reaches out spontaneously to touch his face after she knows he is lost to her, and he does not react.

Lucille's own position as a figure of difference goes beyond gender distinctions involving her role as mother in an otherwise male family. The first time the FBI agent visits the house, he finds her in the yard behind a laundry clothesline, wearing a paper Indian headdress. The moment is played for comic effect, with a cut to a close-up timed with her pulling back a sheet to reveal herself in the risible getup before she explains that she has been playing "Cowboys and Indians" with the neighbor children. Later, when she receives a kimono from her sons in Korea, she dons it eagerly and does a stereotypical Madame Butterfly impersonation in front of the mirror, complete with narrowed eyes, jerky shoulders, and upwardly jutting fingers while the soundtrack thrums with a few grating bars of Orientalist music. Lucille's own fantasies of otherness have a mimetic rather than strictly projective edge, enacting these stereotypes as if to play out their congruency with her own disempowerment.

Indeed, her gestures throughout the film are both performative and imitative, sometimes ironically enacting an authority that is denied to her—as when she shoos the men into the car while they pay no attention—and sometimes playing out her actual abjection, as when, in response to her husband's condescension, she bites her glove, bobs her head, bats her eyes, and pants like a dog. Early in the film as Lucille chants the title rhyme to her son—"Diddle diddle dumpling, my son John"—she also acts it out, bouncing on the bed while cradling her arms around an invisible infant and swinging them to and fro. After the revelation of John's betrayal, the gestural aspect of Hayes's performance recedes as Lucille sinks into despond, yet this mimetic edge remains. It surfaces again when she tries to coax John back to the fold by acting out a football game—a uniquely unsuitable bid, since we know that John's difference from his brothers has been cast in terms of his refusal to participate with them in that presumably all-American ritual. Like so much in the film's last third, the scene is both grotesque and weirdly moving, as Lucille's zonked-out desperation evokes what theorists from Sigmund Freud to Erving Goffman have viewed as a primal function of imitation in the psychic sphere of everyday life—to make the absent present and so compensate for loss.

Such dual identifications as those that *My Son John* encourage for Lucille and John are not uncommon in Classical Hollywood but are usually associated with the romantic couple, with whom we engage individually and jointly in part because of their connections to each other. Here too a mutual identification guides spectators' shifting relations to the characters. The moment that seals our identification with Lucille is her private act of resistance when she stows away the prescribed pills instead of taking them. This is also the moment that consolidates our growing awareness of Lucille's marginalization and her own relation to it. That John shares this knowledge siphons a share of these energies in his direction. If these are subsequently tempered by Lucille's own suspicions, they are reinforced in the extraordinary scene where John outlines his beliefs and Lucille affirms their ideological accord. "I love humanity—the downtrodden, the helpless minorities," John says, to which Lucille responds with a gung ho, "Me too!" This is certainly a turning point in the long run, since it implicates Lucille, our most consistent focal point, in the very belief system the film must ultimately excoriate.

Oedipus, Hollywood, and Cold War ideology

The cornerstone of the film's critique of Cold War domestic ideology is its portrait of the father. No commentator on the film has ever missed the strongly negative cast of this depiction. Even Warshow understands that the father is portrayed as "monstrous," a "pillar of the American Legion presented as so outrageously bigoted, so hopelessly benighted, that one fails to understand why the Legion has not organized a boycott of the film"[13]—as it had in 1949, not incidentally, of *Give Us This Day*, a film by a then-blacklisted director, Edward Dmytryk, who later revived his Hollywood career by appearing as a friendly witness and naming names before HUAC. Dan Jefferson is portrayed at every turn as a small-minded, hypocritical, grand-standing know-nothing, his one saving grace, his affection for Lucille, so mired in patriarchal privilege that it might be a source of distress more grievous than any son's defection. The refusal to laud this character or make him available as a site of viewer identification is the film's staunchest commitment. Indeed, his depiction solidifies the crucial compact among John, Lucille, and the spectator, more than justifying John's subtle ridicule of family politics. Though Lucille expresses some disapproval of this mockery, the film makes clear that she understands it as implicitly as John understands his own place in the prevailing structure. When Dan recites an absurdly jingoistic jingle—"If you don't like your Uncle Sammy, then go back to your home o'er the sea!"—a rare close-up reaction shot emphatically registers her unease and her surreptitious sidelong glance to monitor John's reaction to the appalling spectacle, a response shown in a countershot to be far more successfully contained than her own.

The characterization of Dan Jefferson is unusually intricate, a series of minor foibles gathering slowly into a wholesale indictment, with the slyness of a comedy of manners, detailing the petty mores of a social type bit by bit until the skein of this anatomy suddenly tightens into outright condemnation. The first exhibit is a doddering insecurity that enervates everyone in his orbit while being constantly projected onto them, especially Lucille. From that point, nearly everything Dan does is weighted with the tug of the film's slowly mounting opprobrium. His reaction to a glimpse of John in a distant embrace with his mentor is tritely jealous and grossly excessive—not to mention homophobic, as any contemporary viewer would almost certainly observe—as he spits at the sight of it. ("I thought they were going to kiss!" he sputters.) His crashing the car during the subsequent rant evinces symptoms more dangerous than any that the supposedly medication-worthy Lucille ever presents. His behavior regarding the speech to the Legion is simply petulant, and what we hear of the speech itself is plainly fatuous, rife with the "good old American bromides" that John seems quite right, under the circumstances, to chide. Dan's bullheaded refusal to consider John's suggestions for revision counterpoint his childishness against John's maturity. When John discreetly points out an instance of outright plagiarism in the text, the film plants one of its most pointed jokes at Dan's expense. "I copied it right!" he declares self-righteously. His own accounts of his work as a teacher suggest professional incompetence to boot, as he airs his dyspeptic suspicions that one of his students is a "stool pigeon" who has "snitched" on him for mentioning God in the classroom. The scene implies that Dan has violated a local ordinance in place prior to the federal ban against all prayer in public schools in the United States in 1962. That the film's chief spokesperson against Communism is so thoroughly discredited on every other ground does no favors, of course, for the film's own espousals of that position.

By no means is the film's Oedipal resonance an unusual feature in the context of Classical Hollywood. Indeed, a main current of post-auteurist film theory courted the idea that Oedipal energies formed the basic impulses of Classical Hollywood narrative.[14] Even in the absence of actual fathers, as in Raymond Bellour's main test case, Hitchcock's *North by Northwest* (1959), symbolic ones abound, and the male protagonist's prescribed and predetermined trajectory is to overcome these antagonists and ultimately replace them, much as Freud's mythical offspring were supposed to reconcile hostile and rivalrous paternal feelings in order to achieve identification with the father and thence assume their proper place in the reproductive order, or else endure besetting complexes ever after. It is this dynamic that bodies forth, in turn, the male as active driver of the typical Hollywood narrative, the woman as passive subordinate object of the controlling male gaze. Readings based on this template tend to view any narrative goal—from marriage to avenging the death of the father, getting the stagecoach to Lordsburg, or getting out of Casablanca—as tantamount to achieving (or, much more rarely, failing to achieve) a coveted symbolic fatherhood, with women coming along, as it were, just for the ride. It is worth noting that auteurism itself had an Oedipal tinge to it, in its aspiration to overcome a dominant Tradition of Quality that was also dubbed "le cinéma de papa." Its emerging canon

was awash in absurd, ineffectual, or monstrous fathers, from
Night of the Hunter to *Rebel Without a Cause* and *Bigger than
Life* or Minnelli's melodramas of the late 1950s like *Tea and
Sympathy* (1956) and *Home from the Hill* (1960).

Under this theory, the marriage plot that governs a majority
of Hollywood films inevitably activates the Oedipal trajectory,
so McCarey's lack of interest in any but the most posterior
variants of that narrative should also presumably have the
effect of banishing Oedipus to the background. Indeed, fathers
or father-figures are few and far between in McCarey's films,
which are closer to the Rip van Winkle/Leslie Fiedler line of
American culture, emphasizing male flights from the adult
responsibility that marriage allegedly epitomizes. McCarey's
films are filled with hen-pecked husbands fleeing oppressive
marriages (Laurel and Hardy), avatars of the pleasure principle
steadfastly avoiding them (the lecherous but marriage-phobic
Groucho Marx or the sultry but un-weddable Mae West),
or sundry singles inclined to defer the inevitable as long as
possible and usually tacitly applauded for that impulse. *Make
Way for Tomorrow* is something like Oedipus in reverse,
with a passive, marginalized father nursing grudges against
his oblivious children for putting him out to pasture. Far
from looming as the psychic despot of the domestic imago,
he cannot fail to notice that he and his marriage matter to
his children hardly a whit. A similar indifference attends the
treatment of the father/son relationship in *Going My Way*.
Amused and friendly rather than contentious, the son treats
the father with a briskly affable manner even while obviously
recognizing him as a callous moneygrubber, declining to follow
in his footsteps, and cheerfully announcing radical plans for
his own future—marrying a former prostitute and going off
to war—with no consultation and no concern for his father's
approval, rendering the old man mute with shock, as noted in
a pointed reaction shot that is both comic and poignant.

The most positive depiction of fatherhood and family life
in McCarey appears in *Good Sam*, but the moral of that story
all but demands in the end that the family accept the father's

neglect as he bestows his generosity on others. Sam's most outrageous benefaction is to give a large sum earmarked for the family's new home to a struggling young couple to fund the birth of their child; when a disbelieving Lu learns of the donation, Sam avers, "Well—don't you want children to be born?" Dunderheaded yet ostensibly lovable, the rhetorical question comes right from the heart of McCarey's work, with its irresistible love of children and its irrevocable distaste for networks and institutions of reproduction. The breezy tone encourages us to indulge Sam, with the implication that it is better to be a magnanimous dope than a soulless mercenary. But there is no implication here or elsewhere in McCarey's oeuvre that a father is something anyone with sense would ever wish to be.

Dan Jefferson is the most fully sketched father in McCarey's films and the least sympathetic by far, though a conflicted attitude toward him ultimately circumscribes some of the film's most pressing critical problems. On the one hand, the Oedipal nexus is short-circuited almost as soon as it is broached, the conflicts between father and son being internecine and ideological rather than primal or obviously libidinal. Despite its emotional intensity, the film is as free as any McCarey film of the Freudian melodramatics of a Hitchcock or Minnelli, or the sadomasochistic overtones of a Preminger, Ray, or Sternberg. There is strikingly little sense of John's being in psychic thrall to the family; on the contrary, he relies cannily on vestiges of a past bond to present a modulated appearance of connection while maintaining a cultivated distance tempered by impatience with the parents' persisting claims on him. It is this very detachment that is the cause of Lucille's final despair, together with her realization that he has removed himself in the service of affiliations that are profoundly foreign to her in part because they have trumped the supposedly primal ones.

On the other hand, almost as soon as the film has filed its relentless brief against the father, it finds itself in the untenable position of having to validate him. "You were right all along," Lucille says to Dan, finally convinced of her son's guilt, "because you thought with your heart." Despite the clear turn the line marks, it is worth noting that Dan is still in the dark about John's culpability, and Lucille does not enlighten him. In fact, he continues to express remorse about his suspicions and his squabble with his son, indicating that the import of his wife's pronouncement is lost on him. The scene is as much about the emotional disconnect between them as about Lucille's defeated affirmation of his righteousness. Dan appears not even to notice his wife's near-catatonic despondency, retaining his obliviousness to the end, and from this point on, the film loses all interest in him as a character. Up to this point, he has been treated with a certain mortified fascination, but once his positions must be endorsed, he is reduced to the status of a cipher, resuming his thankless role as nursemaid to his wife. So uninterested does the film become in him that it never bothers to show his reaction to the revelation that his son really is a Communist agent.

The Cold War leavened Hollywood's Oedipal structures in significant ways. The rise of the national-security state required the sanctification of the traditional family because that was in large part what it claimed to be protecting. At the same time, just as all expansions of state power subsumed a share of fatherly authority, it mitigated paternal power just as adult males in America were transmuting into so many Organization Men in Gray Flannel Suits amid the Lonely Crowd, as sociologists of the day diagnosed the conformist tendencies of the time. Domestic ideology had typically arrogated social and economic power to men and moral authority in the home to women, who presumably accepted this division of labor—and their own political disenfranchisement—in exchange for this prerogative. As the Cold War consensus homogenized the middle classes into avid consumers and dutiful red-baiters, concerns about excessive motherly influence emerged in the public sphere. As early as 1942, in the influential best-seller *A Generation of Vipers*, Philip Wylie condemned a cult of motherhood he denigrated as "Momism," based on the fear that the sweetly matronly figure we adored could also be a shrewish harridan in disguise, requiring the worship of submissive husbands and dependent children as well as demanding a steady supply of the latest cosmetics and household appliances. This demonic figure, Wylie cautioned as the Second World War was in full sway, was unlikely to produce good soldiers among her enfeebled offspring, and when Wylie issued a revised and updated edition of the book in 1955, at the height of the Cold War, it was no surprise to find him warning that the nation's mothers, like its washrooms, might be breeding Bolsheviks.

In his acute survey of Cold War cinema, Michael Rogin finds Momism flourishing from *My Son John* and *Pickup on South Street* (1953) to *The Manchurian Candidate*. Rogin acknowledges that *My Son John* presents the American family "through John's detached, discredited eyes" and "exposes [the father's] American Legion costume and his simple-minded patriotic slogans to ridicule"[15] Yet according to Rogin, John becomes a Communist due to his mother's liberal ideas and sexual availability, and he claims that the film highlights the lack of boundaries between them. Though whiffs of Momism waft undeniably through the film, Rogin's own admission of John's detachment highlights that character's insistence on the boundaries the family would deny and his resistance to parental influence. In one of the film's most discomfiting and stringently funny lines, John answers his mother's prim inquiries about his love life with the tart rejoinder, "Sentimentalizing over the biological urge isn't really a guarantee of human happiness, dear." Momism conjured the threat that the sons' desires, instead of being directed toward another woman, would be channeled into sentimental adulation of the mother. As Rogin notes himself, John betrays his mother for a female spy. Rogin accounts for the discrepancy by arguing that John has internalized his mother's naïve humanitarianism and then pointedly distanced himself from her by taking it in a sinister direction. He does not note the film's emphasis on John's renewed identification with the figure of the mother as the route to his repudiation of Communism in the end.

As suggestive as Rogin's discussion is, and as indispensable in placing the film in its Cold War context, his essay is a test case of a piece attuned to social and cultural implications at the expense of authorial ramifications to the detriment of its analysis. Though Rogin pursues a glancing auteurist treatment of Sternberg's *Jet Pilot* (released in 1957), comparing the chemistry in that film between Janet Leigh and John Wayne to the psychodynamics of Sternberg's films with Marlene Dietrich in the 1930s, he brings no awareness of McCarey's work to his discussion of *My Son John*—perhaps because that work is so much less congenial to psychoanalytic interpretation than the bulk of auteur cinema. Rogin brings a cogency to bear that becomes, however admirable in theory, a potential liability in approaching films as oblique in exposition and as resistant to neat formulations as McCarey's, to say nothing of a film as cross-grained as *My Son John*, with its heady, baffling mixture of a sophistication so hard to define with turbulent, flashing infusions of emotional and ideological crudity. Putting aside the commentary on Momism, even Rogin's more literal claims seem somewhat out of keeping with the temper of the film; he asserts flatly that John's mother turns him in to the FBI. This is not exactly wrong (nor exactly right)—but would any careful viewer freed from requirements of rhetorical incisiveness put it that way, given the muffled motivations the film pivots on, or the edgy, crablike motion of the plot, in which turning points are often receding by the time the viewer has discerned them? "In Leo McCarey's technological version of modern Catholic anti-Communism," Rogin declares, with his characteristic manner of pinpointing cruxes, in his one reference to the director, "tape recorder equals mystic body and tape equals soul."[16] As an observation about the film this one is credible and suggestive, but what a student of McCarey would likely be thinking about is how wildly out of character the last scene of *My Son John* is. Nobody trying to account for the film in the context of McCarey's body of work would arrive at such an insight through that route, so alien is the rhetoric of mysticism to his oeuvre and so complicated are the film's own shifting logics.

Contingencies of the uncanny

The last segment of *My Son John* bears a deeply problematic relation to the rest of the film as well as to the rest of McCarey's work, though the latter helps to account for it. In tracing the arc from the shot of John's empty chair at the beginning to that of the vacant podium at the end, the film comes up against an intractable reality: the death of Robert Walker. In McCarey's ideal version, Walker would have stood where that vacancy looms since, in the original conception, the character was not intended to die; in the digital age, he could have stood there, just as a later Walker—Paul—completed his role in *Furious 7* (2015) in computer-generated form after his passing. But even though McCarey did draw upon cinematic resources to construct the illusion of Robert Walker's continued presence onscreen after his sudden death, the character he played transforms into a ghostly figure as the film winds to its end. Three strands are interwoven in this final section: Lucille's breakdown, John's metamorphosis into a figure of the uncanny, and the film's own breakdown, foundering upon contingencies of loss.

Is there a moment in the film when this loss—a young man's departure from life at a particular moment in real time—becomes somehow visible? In a sense, the film is a series of affective ruptures from the start; we could say that these take on a more formal dimension in the end. A haunting shot of Walker in his last scene with Hayes illustrates the shift. In the ordinary logic of film syntax, the shot plays as a reverse-angle, already a bit jarring considering the director's customary avoidance of them. But beyond that something seems off, there is subliminal incongruity, the sense of the shot's deriving from a different order, a separateness in time and space. The shot is too brief, cut off just as Walker's lips begin to move soundlessly. Like much in this final segment, this seems like a disorienting glitch, but there is at least one precedent in McCarey that is unpressured by happenstance. In *Going My Way*, after the banker's son has delivered the news of his marriage and impending departure for war, he takes his leave with the chipper assurance that his father will come to love his new daughter-in-law. It is all very sudden: the amiable reveal as the son quickly dons his military uniform, the son's swift leave-taking. Then there is a shot of the wife, warmly smiling, followed by a reverse-shot of the father, looking flummoxed. He starts to murmur inaudibly as the shot abruptly fades. What does he mean to say, and why make such an issue of his straining to speak at all if only to foreclose his words? It is one of the strangest and most pleasurable shots in the film—an image of the father struck dumb, getting his due, the comeuppance that Dan Jefferson could never receive, like the comeuppance of the son in *The Magnificent Ambersons*, whose own lips, when we see him for the last time, are moving in silent prayer. Yet this moment is not unkind; until Dan, even the fathers in McCarey are treated with a certain gentleness. What the shot tells us is that the father probably *will* be able to love his son's wife, that he is coming at last into himself, becoming what he "really is," a loving father—and that is where we leave him.

What would John say in this moment, if he were enabled to speak? Literally, the shot must be an insert pulled from another scene or even a different Walker performance, cut in after Walker's death with the soundtrack erased. Narratively, it suggests John's softening toward his parents—improbably enough, coming so soon after he has intoned his single line of clichéd villainy: "What are you going to do to stop me?" The shot is infused with suggestions of pity, an initial yielding to his mother's claims on him, laying the groundwork for his subsequent renunciation of Communism. Formally, it initiates the uncanny dissociation between voice and body that shapes the film's portrayal of John for the rest of the film. A subsequent shot shows him in an airport telephone booth, his mouth working frantically, with his speech again occluded. Instead, McCarey cuts to Stedman's office, where we infer John's surrender from the agent's solicitous replies. Finally, in the last scene, John's voice from the tape recorder reverberates through the hall, as if such sonic fullness might somehow compensate for the absence of his body.

A series of shots of Lucille rhyme with these images of John, animating a similar dialectic of absence and presence around voice and voiceless-ness. The first takes place outside the church where she has come to retrieve a pair of her son's pants, donated to a charity drive, that John now mysteriously requests be returned to him. For her pains the priest calls her an "Indian giver," recalling the image of Lucille bedecked in the paper headdress and her role as a conduit to a deracinated "otherness." Until this point she has replied to such jokes in kind, with genial teasing of her own. Now she is rendered mute— the shot of the speechless father in *Going My Way* rendered in desolate negative—because she has found something in the pockets. Later we will learn that it is the key to the apartment of the female spy, but here McCarey withholds the Hitchcockian cut-in, the quicksilver close-up of the MacGuffin, so we do not yet know what she has discovered. This abstention casts her grief in stark abstraction, facing us with the image of her emotional devastation without knowledge of its source. A wordless final long shot shows her shambling away into the distance, her slow gait disconcertingly off-stride, her head bowed as she disappears into a bright gray twilight glare.

The following shots in Washington DC intensify this representation of her inconsolable state—the bereft meeting in John's office, the fugitive riverside encounter with Stedman, the wary trek to Ruth Coplin's apartment. The city's patriotic memorials and towers serve none of their usual functions to provide solace. Rather, they seem to mock Lucille's grief in their galling ubiquity, especially in the riverside scene, where they are inelegantly back-projected, giving them a stylized aspect and furthering the dissociative logic that begins to overtake the film. The agonizing journey to the apartment is a film-with-the-film with the conceit that we are watching through the FBI's surveillance cameras. Before this, Lucille has been the only character to raise objections to the agency's invasiveness. On Stedman's second visit to the house, she points out irately her right to be free of FBI interference. These images of Lucille fixed under the gaze of the surveillance state intrude on her grief even if we assume that the film embraces such technology as necessary to the goal of counter-subversion. The exterior shots are blanched with oversaturated sunlight as Lucille, her laborious motion a slow, depleted trudge, moves through teeming streets more suggestive of urban blight than of the city's fabled monumentalism. The shots are silent, the FBI's technology apparently lacking sound, accompanied by Stedman's ostensibly sympathetic voice-over narrating her journey, his voice standing in for hers as it did for John's, anticipating the outcome of her quest for an answer to the Hitchcockian question *Will the key fit?*—the same query that does indeed resolve the plot of a Hitchcock film three years later, *Dial M for Murder*. At the height of her grief, Lucille is deprived of voice; at the height of John's expiation, all he has is voice.

The silent shot of John in the phone booth revives the spirit of Bruno Anthony in a more literal sense than that in which the entire film is haunted by the ghost of Walker and Hitchcock's character. In that case, McCarey optically printed footage of Walker from *Strangers on a Train* behind the glass in a shot of an empty phone booth. He did the same thing in the scene of John's death, printing shots from Bruno's death scene behind the fractured glass of the overturned car's passenger window. Apparently meant to insulate the shots, to conceal their second-generation status and mask any technical imperfections in the transposition, the translucent surface of the shots imparts a stilled, stranded quality, as of a specimen preserved under glass for heightened scrutiny. In both cases, Walker is immobilized, stuck in the phone booth and trapped in the car, just as Bruno was pinned beneath the collapsed carousel in *Strangers*. In the latter case, fragments of Walker's dialogue from Bruno's death scene were imported into *My Son John*, combined with other lines previously recorded by Walker as well as intonations provided by McCarey himself, multiplying the uncanny effects.

This sequence is the film's most obvious lurch into the territory of the surreal. Stedman stands over the toppled car peering into the window rather as if he were gazing down into

the screen of a kinetoscope. The reverse-shot shows John's/
Walker's/Bruno's superimposed face, its placement suggesting
a bodily position defying laws of space and physics, as it is
difficult to imagine how he could be sprawled in quite this
way between the car's front and back seats. These furnishings,
in any case, have been erased, so that the car's darkened
interior—in broad daylight—has a subterranean look, the face
floating in a blanked-out space, disembodied. As with most of
the posthumous inserts of Walker, this one has an especially
erratic quality due to a tension between the necessity to show
it, to demonstrate John's physical presence in the space of the
film, and the compulsion to cut away to disguise verbal and
visual asynchrony. Though voice and body roughly coincide
in this scene, the dialogue often mismatches the movement
of the actor's lips; the lines we hear are obviously dubbed,
differing at times from the ones he spoke while being filmed.
The scene crystallizes the overdetermination of the conclusion
in its narrative requirement to establish John's repentance and
enable him to inform Stedman where to find the recording of
his speech. McCarey willfully presses the scene's structure to
integrate dialogue from the *Strangers on a Train* sequence. For
example, with comic improbability, Stedman asks if John has
the tape of the speech, enabling John to reply with Bruno's
line, "I haven't got it." Though perhaps meant to smooth out
the incongruities, the effect is weirdly dissonant. In Bruno's
death scene, he refuses to give evidence that would clear Guy,
whom he has framed for his own crime. Walker plays the scene
with an unforgettable mix of Bruno's usual vitriolic derision
and a resigned serenity, since Bruno knows he is dying. In the
line in question—"I haven't got it, it's on the island where
you left it"—the pronoun refers to an incriminating cigarette
lighter that Bruno holds but refuses to surrender. Walker
delivers the line with a breathy, taunting faux-innocence. The
line retains that shading in *My Son John*, giving the scene a
decidedly creepy intonation heightened by its clipped manner,
due to McCarey's need to cut abruptly to elide the subsequent
phrase.

In spasms of techno-idealism, early commentators on film celebrated its capacity to overcome mortality. "[I]t will be possible," mused one spectator, "to see one's loved ones active long after they have passed away," while another proclaimed that once movie cameras were available to the public, "when everyone can photograph their dear ones, no longer in a motionless form but in their movements, death will have ceased to be absolute."[17] André Bazin was not the only theorist to distinguish photography from cinema on the basis of a contrast between stillness and motion, with the former expressing an affinity with death that the animated character of cinema could allegedly transcend. Certainly, a fundamental, persisting fascination with moving images lies in their mechanical ability to chronicle, store, archive, or otherwise preserve representations of movement, duration, and change. Yet this talk of transcendence requires a willed denial of the negativity of finitude and a pronounced *dis*-identification with the dead. With a greater awareness of the liability of visual texts themselves to degradation and loss, more recent theorists highlight precisely the uncanny side of film's preservationist aspects. Mary Ann Doane emphasizes contingencies that both heighten film's power to grasp reality, capturing unanticipated phenomena, and stand against this rhetoric of transcendence by dint of the ungovernable qualities of these phenomena.[18] Laura Mulvey contends that features of new technologies like the "pause" button on video players return stillness to the cinema, revealing the deathlike conditions of photography to be yet contained within the moving image as well. Her own definitions of the uncanny seem especially germane to the case of *My Son John*; it entails, she argues, an "overwhelming or irrational sense of fate or destiny, of an outside intervention into the everyday"; or again, "a disordering of the sensible in the face of sudden disorientation."[19]

My Son John is among the small number of films in which an actor in a movie died before its first release. The effect of such a film is different in theory from, say, the experience of seeing a film made in the distant past with the knowledge that all of its players are no longer living. Walker's unexpected death casts a poignant shadow over *My Son John* much like the one that James Dean's passing cast over his posthumous films. That Walker never entered the realm of "legend" that Dean came to inhabit in part because of his early death could be seen to heighten that poignancy, amplifying the sense of a loss insufficiently mourned. It is striking to note how little Eric Rohmer has to say about Dean's death in his review of *Rebel Without a Cause*, considering the auteurist concern with the nexus between creative will and technological, incidental contingencies in cinema. In that case, Rohmer takes the opportunity to reify the modern image of fate, which is no simple accident like the one that killed Dean but, despite its apparently reduced circumstances, still something closer to the grandeur of tragedy.

Walker's death sealed the fate of the character he played, who had to die only because Walker did. With this factor in mind, the overdetermination of the film's last sections—their almost hysterically willed yet accidental character, the sense of things happening by rote in a restless trance only because they must, even though nobody would have had them turn out quite this way—remains strangely moving even at its most risible. We cannot know exactly what the original conception for the ending was, because the last thirty pages have been removed from archived copies of scripts, evidently as part of McCarey's efforts to conceal the fact that the film had not been completed upon Walker's death. On the contrary, in publicity at the time, he claimed that it was, only later acknowledging the makeshift work of the ending and the fortunate happenstance of Walker's having asked to record the final speech the week before his death, prior to the shooting of the last scene. In these final scenes, a quality of stark desperation unfurls alongside many other affects. The film doubles down on its own newfound convictions with such force that they bear almost no resemblance to its previously hovering, ambiguous subtexts, even as it flails frantically in search of a viable conclusion.

Even this outcome is not without precedent in McCarey's work. The closest of his previous films to *My Son John* in this quality of overdetermination and in this veering among emotional and ideological positions is also the only other one that could plausibly be called "political" and the only other one in which a sense of mortality prevails. *Once Upon a Honeymoon* stands alongside the most important antifascist American films of the day, Chaplin's *The Great Dictator* (1940) and Lubitsch's *To Be or Not to Be* (1942), as a Hollywood comedy about the unlikely subject of Nazism. Both Lubitsch and Chaplin were criticized for trivializing the Fascist threat, and Chaplin himself expressed regret over the satiric treatment he adopted once the horrors of the death camps had been fully revealed. A resounding financial success, *Once Upon a Honeymoon* largely escaped this censure, even though it was released after the American war effort against Fascism was under way, while *The Great Dictator* came out before the United States entered the war and *To Be or Not to Be* only three months after. Of the three films, McCarey's is by far the least concerned with dictates of good taste and the least of a piece as a whole, the least worked-through in balancing its comic elements with its more serious overtones. As a result, incongruous tones clash repeatedly throughout the film. Indeed, *Once Upon a Honeymoon* does not shrink from juxtaposing scenes of rollicking humor with others of considerable gravity, more forthright and disturbing in their depiction of Nazi imagery than anything in Chaplin or Lubitsch, including a hellish vision of a concentration camp following soon after a lighthearted colloquy. The film's propensity to career between these modes is its defining quality, divided among the determination to show the horrors of Nazism in as unvarnished a form as Hollywood would allow, and the obligation to ridicule Nazi ideology while reinforcing aboveboard Americanness. *Once Upon a Honeymoon* features what may be the most violent death scene in a Hollywood film up to that point in depicting the assassination of an American double-agent, a murder shown in full blood-and-gore detail at a time when such representations were effectively banned by the industry's production code. In its way, the film is McCarey's most sustained exploration of abruptness, of the effects of suddenly clashing feeling, as an aesthetic mode.

These scenes are doubly shocking in the context of McCarey's work, with its lightness of surface undergirded by an abiding melancholy—a virtual requirement for auteurs working in a comic mode. We should recall that for the *Cahiers* auteurists, the whiff of mortality pervaded even Hawksian comedy, for example; it was this overtone that kept his work (or Chaplin's, or Keaton's, or Wilder's, or even Tashlin's) from frivolity. The body's mortality is a central theme of such auteurs as Hitchcock or Welles (or indeed, most of the first wave), and when a favored director exhibited an unseemly blithesomeness—as in Minnelli's early work, say—an undercurrent of dejection was always a welcome mitigating circumstance; consider, for instance, the youngest daughter's obsessions with death in that sunniest of auteurist landmarks, *Meet Me in St. Louis* (1944), or the nightmare scene in *Father of the Bride* (1950). Even Capra's predominant cheer is shadowed by a depressive edge, the specter of mortality never very remote—as in the sudden collapse of a boy's mother during an exuberant singalong on a bus in *It Happened One Night* (1934), the kindly murders by the maiden aunts in *Arsenic and Old Lace* (1944), or the plots predicated on suicide of *Meet John Doe* (1941) or *It's a Wonderful Life* (1946).

McCarey's melancholy is of a different stripe, the sting of death very little felt in his films as a whole. That John was not earmarked for death in the original script bolsters the point. The only death in a McCarey film before *Once Upon a Honeymoon* and *My Son John* is that of the grandmother in *Love Affair*, and her passing happens off-screen, in the narrative past of the story, registered sadly but with a strikingly matter-of-fact sense of simple, death-be-not-proud acceptance. In the same film, the threat of death looms when Terry is struck off-screen by a car, but McCarey hurries past this crisis with a tonic briskness to the reassurance of her survival. Later, in *The Bells of St. Mary's*, he mocks the melodrama of that scene in a genial self-parody: after the benefactor resolves to release his lien on the church, just as he leaves to finalize this arrangement, an off-screen screech of tires sounds, just like the one in *Love Affair*, but a whimsical subsequent shot shows him crouched in the street under the stopped vehicle, waving buoyantly and declaring himself unharmed. In neither case is the threat of mortality allowed much force. For a film about the alleged desolations of old age, too, *Make Way for Tomorrow* is surprisingly free of that threat. In the novel that the film is based on, the husband sickens and dies in a tear-jerking turning point near the book's end; McCarey removes this incident from the adaptation, makes Bark a much heartier character, and never encourages us to fear the prospects of death for either of the main characters despite their advanced age.

This reading may stake a minority position. In his sensitively nuanced overview of McCarey's career in *Romantic Comedy in Hollywood*, James Harvey finds, on the contrary, that *Make Way for Tomorrow* "dwells almost obsessively on just the kind of event the romantic comedy is obliged to omit: aging and dying and children who grow up to be awful."[20] At best, however, Harvey is speaking of mortality as an abstraction, even a metaphor. Later, he argues that McCarey possesses a knowledge denied to one such as Capra that "makes [McCarey] a deeper—and a funnier—artist than Capra is"— namely, "the fact that we can like each other quite a lot, really and even deeply—and *still* do each other in."[21] That emotional pain underlies the comedy of both Capra and McCarey in different ways (as well as much comedy *tout court*) seems undeniable; even so, the obsessiveness Harvey imputes, though a useful attribute for any auteur, seems at odds with both the pragmatism and the restiveness of the work, its tendency to flit from mood to mood and to evade its own implications. This is not to say, of course, that subtexts do not crucially inflect McCarey's films; they are definitive. There can be no question that McCarey's work even in its romantic-comedy mode underlines the ache of love—as opposed to its agony or torment, which a really death-obsessed auteur like Bergman explores—and the destructiveness of social controls upon it. But especially considering the distinctive temporality of his films—the lag-and-lurch, the too-long moments, the quick note and the long haul, the feeling of having to wait out an excruciating perpetuity—the sense of melancholy derives more from having to *live* with disillusionment and alienation than having to die from them. McCarey's melancholy may be the result of an unfulfilled mourning, as Freud says melancholy always is, but the films suggest that what he's in mourning for (like the character in Chekhov) is life.

Walker's death denied *My Son John* the "happy" ending McCarey had planned, in which John takes the stage to renounce Communism and embrace parental and godly authority. However one might imagine it, that ending too would seem to break with what preceded it. The film confronts us with a classic conundrum of narrative closure. Do we read backward from what has come before, or forward from what has been established? The question is especially pressing here because the ending of *My Son John* partakes of both the predetermination and structural pressure of the "closed" text, satisfying demands of resolution, and the emotional climate of the "open" text, with its sense of suspension and incompletion.[22] Narrative theorists tend on the whole to prefer the latter type because it enables the reader/spectator's freedom to interpret as well as honoring the open destinies of life, but this privileging of the ending itself leaves open the question of how narrative segments interact. Does an unsatisfying ending entirely "undo" the work that it concludes? Does the simplifying, tacked-on resolution of *The Magnificent Ambersons*, likely the only one we will ever have to that film, cancel the complexities that lead up to it? How does the ironic happy ending of many a Hollywood auteur condition our readings of the films as a whole, even assuming that we grant the irony in the first place, rather than writing it off as a failed attempt at closure? Max Ophuls's *Caught*, for example, ends with the stillborn death of a baby, yet the rhetoric of this conclusion is one of uplift, as we see a close-up of the mother looking radiant and happy in her hospital bed because she knows she is now free of the psychotic father of the dead child. The father has also just suffered a heart attack, so the story could easily have sacrificed him rather than the baby, yet in another stroke of blistering irony, he survives. The "happy" affect depends on our forgetting the baby as much as everyone in the film seems to have done; the irony creeps in if we don't, and experience a deeply bitter aftertaste that, in retrospect, heightens the irony of the film as a whole. Sirk, too, spoke of his efforts to achieve "aporia" in his Hollywood films, that is, to disclose impasses of the text in the act of closure, unresolved elements that would leave the questions of the narrative suspended.[23]

The ending of *My Son John* does lend itself to being read in this tradition, but here, unlike the cases above, a fuller awareness of McCarey's sensibility points against such an interpretation. Though irony plays some localized role in McCarey's films, his work is far from the model of cosmopolitan sophistication and world-weary self-consciousness of the auteurs who rehearsed the ironic happy ending in their Hollywood work (mostly émigrés, like Sirk and Ophuls). An ironic reading of the ending of *My Son John* risks appearing as overdetermined as the ending itself. The matter is complicated further by the narrative peculiarities of McCarey's films, their penchant to place part above whole, to digress unexpectedly, and to divide stories into discrete episodes. In general, these elements convey something of McCarey's explicit stands *against* self-consciousness at a narrative level, creating the strange impression that some scenes in a given film do not know about other scenes in the same film. This accounts for the wildly divergent strains of a film like *Once Upon a Honeymoon*, and it is, if anything, the very *lack* of narrative self-consciousness, the directness and straightforwardness, that allows that film to work this way, if not exactly to cohere in any conventional sense.

The sense of loss that pervades the final scenes of *My Son John* includes the loss of the kind of confidence that makes the boldly shifting tones of *Once Upon a Honeymoon* possible. It stands in opposition to the brash credence that *My Son John* suddenly invests in its anti-Communist message and turns upon the *dis*investment in identifications with John, coinciding—uncannily enough—with John's return to "normality." In some respects, John's final disembodied oration recalls another famous conclusive speech, almost certainly a model for the scene in McCarey, from a film with a close intertextual relation to *Once Upon a Honeymoon*—Chaplin's *The Great Dictator*. Nearly McCareyian in its construction, that film shuttles back and forth between antics involving a Hitler-like despot and his hapless look-alike, a Jewish barber, both played by Chaplin. This setup prods us to expect a mistaken-identity plot that only arrives belatedly, in the final scene, when the barber is mistaken for the dictator and expected to give an address in that guise. Instead of the fascistic ideology the audience expects the dictator to dispense, the barber delivers a gentle, humanistic speech (albeit with overtones of the Popular Front) in favor of freedom and democracy, speaking directly to the camera with a growing intensity that becomes overwhelming. Almost as soon as the speech begins, the barber disappears, replaced by Chaplin himself, who recites the speech with no mediation of a character any longer intervening between himself and the audience. One might be moved by the content of the speech itself, though one might just as easily dismiss it as a compendium of sentimental clichés if conditioned to suspect a knee-jerk humanism. But the directness and the conviction are almost irresistible; the power of the speech lies in its rhetoric more than its content, and when the crowd cheers at the end, instead of dismay at their hypocrisy and fickleness—everything we know tells us they'd have cheered for the dictator just the same, after all—we are more likely to weep at this clear, impassioned message of hope, sent up as a clarion call to arms at the outset of a devastating war.

John's speech too depends on directness and conviction. For the "good old American bromides" John mocks with the film's sanction earlier, it substitutes anti-Communist bromides about the dangers of mind-control and mass manipulation by the state, combined with abject victim-porn ("Nobody warned me as I am warning you ... I played the role they scripted for me ...") and self-recrimination ("Every word is a lie because *I* am a lie, a living lie—a real American traitor ... "). Chaplin's speech evokes ideals of love and compassion with a progressivist slant, so the film's putative ascent into mysticism at this point comes as no surprise, even as abetted by music from the 1850 opera *Lohengrin* by Richard Wagner, an avowed anti-Semite whose music was famously co-opted by the Nazi regime. Chaplin used the same musical source in an earlier scene in which the dictator performs a grotesque dance with a balloon-globe, acting out his puerile fantasies of absolute world domination. This counterpoint yields competing versions of Wagner's transcendental mythos, with an implicit critique of the Fascist co-opting of Wagner.

By contrast with this structural integration, the last scene of McCarey's film is cut off from the rest. It is one of those McCarey scenes that does not seem to know about the existence of the other ones. We know that the speech itself is a lie, if only because it is impossible to imagine John's having grown up in the environment we have witnessed without being "warned" against Communism. The divergence between the scene's intense conviction and its obvious duplicity topples it into kitsch. In its way, the scene is a final gesture toward the abolition of self-consciousness. But the gesture cannot be triumphant, because the film has granted such speculative credibility to self-consciousness beforehand, by way of its erstwhile, ambivalent identifications with John. For much of the film, John's knowingness is an object of curious fascination that the film attempts to understand from its own bluff vantage point (bluff in the sense of good-natured directness, though the opposing sense of deceptiveness is not irrelevant here). That perspective becomes the position of sameness where we end, from which John's difference has been expunged and into which Lucille's has been subsumed. It is a fantasy of ideological homogeneity to end a film that still cannot pride itself fully on being homogenous. The disappearance of John's queerness, its replacement by the normative vacancy from which his speech issues, relates inversely to the film's conclusive sadness. Exactly the opposite of the McCareyian desire, it is just when John becomes what he "really is"—the good, obedient son—that he is lost.

Two last shots sound uncanny McCareyian grace notes: a too-quick cut to Dan and Lucille already making their way up the aisle even before the last word of the speech has subsided and a reverse-shot as they totter into the churchyard to pray for their dead son. "There was a lot of good in what he said," muses Dan as the heavenly choir keens, and Lucille replies, "Let's hope they remember what he said, and not what he did." This platitude is more jarring than others that have cropped up because it draws Lucille herself into the conclusive lie, since neither we nor they know "what he did." Yet this last shot is beautiful, recalling the final close-up in *Ordet*, with a similar ashen sheen and glimmering light, and a similar divide between the grief of the mother and the obtuseness of the father. The sadness we feel at a film is never really *in* the film; the sadness of this one is in part the regret duly summoned in the presence of an auteurist "masterpiece," one quite nearly achieved, that reveals itself almost in full and then, so quickly, departs.

Notes

1   Stanley Cavell, *Pursuits of Happiness: The Hollywood Comedy of Remarriage* (Cambridge: Harvard University Press, 1984), 243.

2   See Thom Andersen, "Red Hollywood," in *"Un-American" Hollywood: Politics and Film in the Blacklist Era*, Frank Krutnick, Peter Stanfield, and Brian Neve, eds. (New Brunswick, NJ: Rutgers University Press, 2007), 225–274.

3   John Lee Mahin, *My Son John*, unpublished treatment dated January 31, 1950, on file in MHL, 3.

4 John Lee Mahin, *My Son John*. Unpublished script dated December 21, 1950, on file at MHL, 71.

5 Leo McCarey, *My Son John,* Myles Connolly, coauthor, unpublished script dated March 30, 1951, on file at MHL, 1.

6 Sergei Eisenstein, *Film Form*, Jay Leyda, trans. (New York: Harcourt, 1969), 57.

7 Bazin, *What is Cinema? Vol. 1,* 148–153.

8 Giorgio Agamben, *Means Without Ends: Notes on Politics* (Minneapolis: University of Minnesota Press, 2000), 49–62. See also Chris Berry, "The New Gestural Cinema," *Film Quarterly* 67, no. 4 (Spring 2014): 17–29.

9 Delmer Daves and Donald Ogden Stewart, *Love Affair,* unpublished script dated December 6, 1938, on file at MHL, 99.

10 Robert Warshow, *The Immediate Experience: Movies, Comics, Theatre and Other Aspects of Popular Culture* (Cambridge: Harvard University Press, 2002), 134.

11 James Baldwin, *The Devil Finds Work* (New York: Dial Press, 1976), 106.

12 Ibid., 105–106.

13 Warshow, *The Immediate Experience*, 135.

14 See Raymond Bellour, *Analysis of Film* Constance Penley, trans. (Bloomington: Indiana University Press, 2001), 90–92. See also Jane Gaines, ed., *Classical Hollywood Narrative: The Paradigm Wars* (Durham, NC: Duke University Press, 1992), 50–52, 189–190.

15 Michael Paul Rogin, "Kiss Me Deadly: Communism, Motherhood, and Cold War Movies," in *Ronald Reagan, the Movie* (Berkeley: University of California Press, 1988), 251.

16 Ibid., 260.

17 Both quoted in Noël Burch, *Life to Those Shadows* (Berkeley: University of California Press, 1990), 21.

18 Mary Ann Doane, *The Emergence of Cinematic Time: Modernity, Contingency, the Archive* (Cambridge: Harvard University Press, 2002), 60–63.

19 Laura Mulvey, *Death 24x a Second: Stillness and the Moving Image* (Islington, UK: Reaktion Books, 2006), 62.

20 James Harvey, *Romantic Comedy in Hollywood: From Lubitsch to Sturges* (New York: Da Capo Press, 1998), 250.

21 Ibid., 257–258.

22 See Richard Neupert, *The End: Narration and Closure in the Cinema* (Detroit, MI: Wayne State University Press, 1995), 35–102–112.

23 Jon Halliday, ed., *Sirk on Sirk* (London: Faber and Faber, 1971), 132.

Conclusion

After auteurism

In 1964, two young Frenchmen traveled to Hollywood, one fat and the other skinny, like Laurel and Hardy. In the hope of ingratiating themselves with the editors of *Cahiers du Cinéma*, they had come to bring the news of auteurism to the auteurs themselves. "America was completely at peace," wrote the skinny one, Serge Daney.[1] The irony that the nation was also at war was not lost on him. In fact, this paradox was what gave the place its character, its sleek, fading luster. The cinema, thought Daney, bore a particular relation to time in which the present was always really the past. Yet the lover of cinema was never the forlorn nostalgist but rather "the one who, watching a film that has just been released, a contemporary film, already feels the passing, the 'that will have been.'" Cinema's perpetual "present" compels not by entombing the past or mummifying change but by deferring the future, holding off its claims to obligation and to the administration of experience. Meanwhile, Daney's predecessors at *Cahiers* were now making films, contributing to the transformation of the cinema into a country in its own right, in which America might be just another principality rather than holding the keys to the kingdom.

The *politique des auteurs* was founded on ideas about cultural time lags and the belatedness of film, an industrial medium that harked back to the nineteenth century for its ideas about sensibility (or even the eighteenth, if D. W. Griffith is the Samuel Richardson of cinema). Writing in the early 1990s, Daney made this connection explicit when he says that what the cinephile craves is an endurance like that of the cinema itself, which persists and decays like a body. He notes that the auteurists loved the Hollywood cinema for its physical energy while also recognizing that it was waning at the very moment they embraced it. A few years after his Hollywood visit Daney found himself standing up in the halls of the University of Paris alongside Pascal Bonitzer, howling that materialist, political cinema was all, with no compromises and Hollywood out of the question. A few years later, "auteur theory" too would be essentially over. We could date its end to 1972, when Peter Wollen adapted it for poststructuralism in the second edition of *Signs and Meaning in the Cinema* only three years after the firmly structuralist-oriented first edition. So altered was Wollen's revision, it hardly made sense to call it "auteur theory" any longer, and in criticism and theory, almost nobody did, though Wollen himself was loath to surrender the phrase. Though it persisted in some senses as critical method, its proponents in theory, always few, went the way of the New Critics as the Sophists had before them.

What happened then was unexpected. The auteur of theory became the auteur of fact, a living, breathing entity, though subject to unusually virulent and prolonged labor pains in the birthing, and rivaling Proteus in restless, mercurial shape-shifting. Daney's trip to Hollywood was a fascinating chapter in this metamorphosis. With his companion Louis Skorecki, Daney looked up as many of the "old-timers" as would see them, to confront them in the flesh, pulling Jacques Tourneur away from his desk at the Directors Guild, visiting Jerry Lewis on the set of an unnamed Frank Tashlin film (the time line supposes it must have been *The Disorderly Orderly* [1964]), meeting George Cukor in a sunny arbor off Sunset Boulevard.

Tourneur greeted them courteously, Lewis rattled a copy of
Cahiers in delight to find himself canonized there, and Cukor
evinced a polite disdain that turned to open derision when
the pair mentioned their admiration for Nicholas Ray's *Wind
Across the Everglades* (1958). Not knowing that Ray was an
auteur any more than he knew he was one himself, Cukor cried
to his minions, "'Come here, come here! You know which film
they like? *Wind Across the Everglades*! That film Jack Warner
wouldn't even dare release!'" Though Ray was still under fifty
when he made it, *Wind Across the Everglades* counts as a late
film; Ray completed only three more in Hollywood after it.
Daney is quite clear that the "late film" is central to auteurism,
especially when it is "exposed to the condescension of official
criticism," bringing any auteurist worth the name running to
the defense of the "old-timers." Occasionally, Daney reports,
he and Skorecki would stumble upon younger filmmakers
who were "more conscious of their situation," like Sam Fuller,
who happily plays the role of crusty auteur for the two French
amateurs. What "situation" were these filmmakers "more
conscious" of? Precisely, that of their being auteurs. The auteurs
had always been defined by *Cahiers* as combining something
intensely *self*-conscious (about the nature of modernity, about
the "logic" of the cinema) with something redemptively *un*-
conscious (sincere, direct, unpretentious, "naïve," and so on).
Daney and Skorecki should hardly have been put off that
the auteurs did not know they were auteurs. What seems to
trouble Daney is the emergence of these younger filmmakers
who *did* know.

   If according to the *politique* an auteur is mainly a Hollywood
director of the first or second generation of sound cinema who
is producing "modern" work that is still *late*, either by virtue
of the director's age or simply by virtue of appearing in the
twilight of the studio system, then there could by rights be no
auteurs in the New Hollywood. By 1968, most of the conditions
that obtained in the "age of the auteurs" had altered or were
changing substantially. The Production Code Administration
was out of business, signaling the end of regulatory practices

that had situated the Hollywood film as the particular kind of conventionalized, stylized artifact the auteurists had cherished. The studio system was transforming from an aggregate of centralized, vertically integrated corporations into a cluster of multinational conglomerates, monopolistic as the studio system had been but so intricately structured, with power diffused so broadly, that it could be difficult to trace chains of command. The top-down organization of the Classical era that had enabled the empowerment of certain creative partners (like auteurs) gave way to a diffuse network of less clearly hierarchical interests asserting claims and counterclaims. Freelance labor increased across all levels, becoming the norm, and supported by a network of agents and managers, held in balance by another network of external guilds and unions. And by the end of the 1970s, in this hectic and decentralized milieu, as the New Hollywood itself began to give way to whatever would follow it, auteurs—though they could not possibly exist there—were suddenly everywhere: the "film generation," the Hollywood brats.

No more than George Cukor welcomed the news that he or Nicholas Ray were auteurs, despite the prestige he could have gained by accepting the moniker, the industry had harbored little hospitality for the idea from the start. Tracing the word "auteur" from the 1960s through the 1990s in *Variety*, the industry's trade paper of record, is an instructive exercise.[2] In one of the earliest references, the same Mike Nichols who would denounce the "froggy conspiracy" forty years later was already on guard as he accepted an award for *The Graduate* (1967), one of the founding texts of the New Hollywood. "At the risk of demolishing the 'auteur' theory, this film was made by a group of people," Nichols said in his acceptance speech. "I can't tell you who did what. I hope I did some of it" (1/31/68, p. 4). Another article in the same issue warns that the auteur theory is invading American universities, pointing to the 1967 "best-of-the-year" list of the *Harvard Crimson*'s film critic (Tim Hunter, who went on to become a director himself) which "included several films admired by *Cahiers*-ists but hardly any other serious critics" (p. 32). (Hunter's eclectic and admirable list was as follows: *El Dorado* [Hawks], *Falstaff* [Welles], *Bonnie and Clyde* [Penn], *La Guerre est Finie* [Resnais], *Hurry Sundown* [Preminger], *Bike Boy* [Andy Warhol], *Chappaqua* [Conrad Rooks], *Accident* [Joseph Losey], *Billion Dollar Brain* [Ken Russell].)

In the late 1960s, *Variety* viewed the "auteur theory" as a clear and present danger. In those early years of the New Hollywood, the paper reported constantly on auteurism in the context of industry labor relations. The screenwriter Philip Dunne declared, "The auteur theory can seriously hurt the writer where it hurts most: in his pocketbook" (10/25/66, p. 66). Auteurism was repeatedly adduced as a cause of disputes among guilds representing film editors, writers, and directors. When the Directors Guild claimed possessive credits, the American Cinema Editors (ACE) union objected, according to an article headlined "Film Editors, Like Writers, Blow Cold on Modern Tout of 'Auteur' Directors" (3/20/68, p. 17). An adjacent article on the same page claimed "Hard Bitten Hollywood Directors Resist That Film Patter," distinguishing between skeptical old Hollywood pros and the younger directors more inclined to embrace this "patter." At a ceremony for the ACE's "Eddie" awards, members of the guild complained publicly that "the director's 'auteur' theory began to be believed in Hollywood" (3/16/70, p. 20). The same year, the Writers' Guild boycotted the first Film Expo festival in Los Angeles because it credited directors over writers in its promotions, with the Guild issuing a letter of protest against the auteur theory, "espoused mostly by film critics who know little about the actual making of films" (11/4/70, p. 1).

Within a few years, however, *Variety* began to refer to auteurs routinely, as if the word had never posed a threat. The film *Electra Glide in Blue* was casually said to have produced "the first auteur ad campaign (by the auteur himself)" (8/29/73, p. 8), for example, while the director Larry Cohen was cited in passing as "the young action auteur" (5/28/75, p. 32). In a conciliatory mood, a spokesperson for the Writers' Guild officially qualified the organization's earlier protest, claiming that they had never really objected to the auteur theory but that the auteur must be worthy of that status as "one who, starting with the initial concept, writes the script, directs and produces the film, and carries through to the final product" (10/28/75, p. 64). This briefly became the industry's semiofficial definition of an "auteur." Nevertheless, *Variety* used the word thereafter interchangeably with "director." Since then the term's expansion has known no bounds, conscripted as an adjective to describe auteur art, auteur photography, auteur music, and a noun that can be modified, it seems, by virtually anything. In a given month, in the culture section of any publication that might come to hand, one encounters references in passing to comedy auteurs (like Rachel Bloom or Phoebe Waller-Bridge), DJ auteurs (like Danger Mouse), music video auteurs (like Anthony Mandler), psych-pop auteurs (like Art Feynman), stage auteurs (like Sam Mendes or Ivo von Hove), TV auteurs (like Shonda Rhimes or Matthew Weiner).

Many old pros and former auteurs kept working into the 1970s, including Hawks and Hitchcock, but the New Hollywood auteurs were Young Turks much as the 1950s auteurists had been, taking as their models films of the French New Wave on the one hand and the classical auteurs on the other, with a feverish counterculture ambience in the mix. Godard, Ford, Hawks, and Hitchcock were the paragons. A quintessential New Hollywood film like Martin Scorsese's *Taxi Driver* (1975) borrowed ideas from Godard movies while recycling a pastiche of Ford's plot from *The Searchers* (1956), inhabiting Hawksian all-male milieus and featuring music by Bernard Herrmann that cited the composer's own scores for Hitchcock. Like the old, the new crop divided between moderately self-reflexive types like Scorsese, Francis Ford Coppola, and Brian De Palma, and mythmakers like George Lucas and Steven Spielberg, even the latter flirting with demystifying impulses that flared briefly, in explicit rejection of old Hollywood attitudes. It was a version of the strain of critique the *Cahiers* writers had located in the work of the 1950s auteurs, but it had turned into a postmodern variant that waned by the end of the decade in favor of a new species of neo-romantic mythmaking allied with post-humanist spectacle (*Star Wars, Indiana Jones, Mission: Impossible,* superhero movies, and so forth).

If the classical/modernist auteur was guilty of pretending to autonomous subjectivity, the New Hollywood auteur was an obvious stand-in for corporate personhood in the postmodern age. As Timothy Corrigan mused considering the celebrity auteur of the New Hollywood, "If auteurism can be used to promote a movie, filmmakers now run the commerce of the auteurist and autonomous self up against its textual expression in a way that shatters the coherence of both authorial expression and stardom."[3] Since this "shattering" was what film theorists had been calling for, it must have been gratifying to find it achieved just as auteurs became flesh-and-blood beings rather than more safely theoretical entities. Yet, in an institutional terrain as riven as that of postclassical Hollywood, as ordered and chaotic simultaneously as anything Foucault ever dreamed of, any auteur would have had to be a "powerful" figure indeed to negotiate it. As Jeff Menne suggests, the New Hollywood auteurs mobilized "personal style" to assert their new authority.[4] They were culture heroes of a new age, the "mavericks" still capable of shaping a vast corporate machinery to persisting auteurist will and delivering their "vision" against all odds. In short, they were everything the anti-auteurists had stood against, except now they knew it.

On the cusp of the New Hollywood, in a shabby studio commissary, Daney and Skorecki met Leo McCarey. Their interview with him would appear the next year in *Cahiers*, along with the essay Skorecki filed under the pen name of Noames, saying McCarey was a dark anarchist, that he regarded life as an obstacle, that his films were populated by strange beasts, that they showed the impossibility of physical love and of being itself. The meeting was disheartening. McCarey slurped yogurt and kept spilling it on himself. He was not, wrote Daney, "a sublime old-timer, he was a sick man, an extremely emaciated has-been, and also very bitter." None of this comes through in the published interview, where McCarey says he had always hoped that someone would come along wondering who was the auteur of those old movies he had worked on. As Daney says, the whole encounter was very "McCareyian" because, like a McCarey film, it was pure awkwardness. This, thought Daney, was all the proof needed for a well-founded *politique des auteurs*.

Notes

1   Serge Daney, *Postcards from the Cinema*, Paul Grant, trans. (New York: Bloomsbury Academic, 2007), 77. All quotations from Daney in the conclusion derive from his account here of his visit to Hollywood, pages 73–77.

2   All quotations in the following two paragraphs come from *Variety*, with issue dates and page numbers given parenthetically.

3   Timothy Corrigan, "Auteurs and the New Hollywood," in *The New American Cinema*, Jon Lewis, ed. (Durham, NC: Duke University Press, 1998), 51.

4   Jeff Menne, "The Cinema of Defection: Auteur Theory and Institutional Life," *Representations* 114, no. 1 (Spring 2011): 36–64.

FURTHER READING

Listed in chronological order of publication

Directed by Dorothy Arzner, by Judith Mayne. Bloomington: Indiana University Press, 1995. This study of the only woman directing films in Hollywood in the 1930s provides an account of authorship that steers clear of pitfalls of auteurism, including its masculinist tendencies. The result is a pioneering work of feminist film scholarship. Also noteworthy is Mayne's 2005 book on Claire Denis in the *Contemporary Film Directors* series (see below).

Authorship and Film, by David A. Gerstner and Janet Staiger. New York: Routledge, 2003. Anthologies about authorship form a virtual genre in film studies, from John Caughie's indispensable *Theories of Authorship* in 1981 to Barry Grant's *Auteurs and Authorship* in 2008. This volume consists mainly of original work rather than previously published material, from the editors' overviews to essays on Michael Curtiz (by Peter Wollen), Joan Harrison (Hitchcock's "assistant"), Oscar Micheaux, John Waters, and others. Most pieces point in new directions for the study of film authorship, including contributions on "poststructural" auteurism, "grassroots authors" in community video, and "discursive authorship" in Asian-American cinema.

Contemporary Film Directors. University of Illinois Press, 2003 - . Inaugurated by James Naremore, this series has produced some of the most incisive books in English on filmmakers of recent years, from Abbas Kiarostami to Jerry Lewis, Agnes Varda, and Edward Yang. Naremore is the author of distinguished studies on the work of Orson Welles, Vincente Minnelli, Stanley Kubrick, and Charles Burnett, each attuned to social and political questions as much as to authorial signatures, and this series follows that model. Of special note recently is Jeff Menne's 2005 *Francis Ford Coppola*, culminating his work on auteurism in the New Hollywood cited elsewhere in this book.

The Death of Classical Cinema: Hitchcock, Lang, Minnelli, by Joe McElhaney. Albany, NY: State University of New York Press, 2008. This study of the late work of these directors places their films against the cultural politics of auteurism as well as examining formal dimensions of authorship. Especially striking is the treatment of the ways in which energies of late classical cinema become diffused in subsequent cinemas, including those with anticlassical inclinations (i.e., the influence of Fritz Lang's Hollywood films on Rivette or Straub-Huillet).

Obscure Invitations: The Persistence of Authorship in Twentieth-Century American Literature. Palo Alto, CA: Stanford University Press, 2011. One of the most original recent treatments of the theory of authorship, this book understands authors' acts as modes of address ("invitations") that are indirect by definition, obscuring their status as communication but not absenting it. The focus is on modernist and postmodern literature but also includes films like *Seven* and *The Usual Suspects* (both films released in 1995).

America's Corporate Art: The Studio Authorship of Hollywood Motion Pictures, by Jerome Christensen. Palo Alto, CA: Stanford University Press, 2012. This major work points beyond auteurism by showing how studios imprint their brands upon even auteur films like *Singin' in the Rain* and *Vertigo*. Voluminously researched, as well versed in critical theory as in industry studies, the book hardly puts the final nail in the coffin of auteurism, since Christensen is a bit of an auteurist himself, as his comments on Hitchcock in the *Vertigo* chapter attest. But the book clearly opens up new directions for thinking about film authorship.

Signs and Meaning in the Cinema, by Peter Wollen. London: British Film Institute, 2013. This is the definitive edition of Wollen's landmark work of film theory, incorporating material from previous editions. The volume also includes fascinating appendices like the series of essays on film directors Wollen wrote in the 1960s under the pen name "Lee Russell" for *New Left Review*. That place of publication suggests that the critique of auteurism as apolitical did not always hold. Wollen's complex sense of auteurism and its ties to the modernist tradition have significantly influenced the present study.

The Life of the Author, by Sarah Kozloff. Montreal: Caboose Publishing, 2014. This book argues strongly for the validity of biographical criticism, ending with a case study of *The Red Kimona* (1925). Drawing on archival research, Kozloff shows how knowledge of the lives of contributors like writer Dorothy Arzner, producer Dorothy Davenport, and director Walter Lang influences a full understanding of the film.

Making Time in Stanley Kubrick's Barry Lyndon: *Art, History, and Empire*, by Maria Pramaggiore. New York: Bloomsbury, 2015. This book provides a model for the extended study of a single film, not only in relation to its director's work but in a bracing variety of other contexts, from the philosophy of time to historical questions of national identity and empire. Though obviously reaching far beyond an auteurist approach, the book also comments trenchantly on the continuing usefulness of auteurism as a critical paradigm.

Impersonal Enunciation, or the Place of Film, by Christian Metz. Cormac Deane, trans. New York: Columbia University Press, 2016. Metz was the key figure in moving French film theory beyond auteurism in the 1960s with his pioneering applications of Saussurean semiotics to the cinema and his subsequent turn to psychoanalytic models. This posthumous volume is a culmination of that work, asking "what speaks" in film and finding the answer to be fascinatingly elusive. Studying the "impersonal" forces of cinematic communication and expression, Metz also offers acute insights into the relation of this dimension to the "personal expression" models of auteurism.

The Elusive Auteur: The Question of Film Authorship Throughout the Age of Cinema, by Barrett Hodsdon. Jefferson, NC: McFarland and Company, 2017. Appearing just as this book went to press, this volume usefully complements the tighter focus of the present project. Comprehensive and encyclopedic, this study traces the permutations of authorship in film from pre-*Cahiers* concepts through the postmodern moment and beyond. Especially interesting work includes sections on the role of cinephilia in the construction of auteurism and the "sublime moment" in auteur cinema, including McCarey's *The Awful Truth*.

INDEX

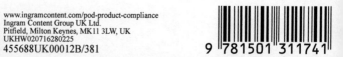